普通高等教育经管类专业"十三五"规划教材

会 计 英 语

景 刚 张 淼 主 编
李佳钰 王文杰 副主编

清华大学出版社
北 京

内 容 简 介

本书是一本为会计英语教学而编写的专业基础教材,内容以基础会计理论、财务会计为主,介绍了资产、负债、所有者权益、收入、费用、利润的会计处理,同时兼顾财务报表及审计的主要内容。该书共有11章,每章由开篇案例、正文、单词注释、拓展阅读、课后练习等组成。通过对本书的学习,读者可以掌握会计学基本理论、基本方法的英语表达方式,对拓展会计专业英文词汇、提高运用英语处理会计业务的能力、阅读会计专业英文文献等大有助益。教材内容充实完整,英文习题丰富齐全,在阐述财务与会计理论和实务方法时,既重视基本理论的深度与广度,又强调具体实务的实际操作方法的运用。选用典型的实例,思路清晰,便于理解。

教材基本素材选自英语原版教材,但表述形式力求符合中国人的思维习惯、价值观念与文化特征,深入浅出、通俗易懂,以适应不同层面学生的学习。本书可作为高等院校本科和高职高专会计、审计、财务管理等专业的会计英语课程教材,也可作为广大财会从业人员学习会计英语的专业书籍。

本书提供配套课件和习题答案,下载地址为 http://www.tupwk.com.cn/downpage。

本书封面贴有清华大学出版社防伪标签,无标签者不得销售。
版权所有,侵权必究。举报: 010-62782989,beiqinquan@tup.tsinghua.edu.cn。

图书在版编目(CIP)数据

会计英语 / 景刚,张淼 主编. —北京: 清华大学出版社,2019(2022.3重印)
(普通高等教育经管类专业"十三五"规划教材)
ISBN 978-7-302-52756-5

Ⅰ. ①会… Ⅱ. ①景… ②张… Ⅲ. ①会计—英语—高等学校—教材 Ⅳ. ①F23

中国版本图书馆 CIP 数据核字(2019)第 071347 号

责任编辑: 崔 伟　马遥遥
封面设计: 周晓亮
版式设计: 方加青
责任校对: 牛艳敏
责任印制: 宋 林

出版发行: 清华大学出版社
网　　址: http://www.tup.com.cn,http://www.wqbook.com
地　　址: 北京清华大学学研大厦A座　　　邮　编: 100084
社 总 机: 010-83470000　　　　　　　　　邮　购: 010-62786544
投稿与读者服务: 010-62776969,c-service@tup.tsinghua.edu.cn
质 量 反 馈: 010-62772015,zhiliang@tup.tsinghua.edu.cn

印 装 者: 北京嘉实印刷有限公司
经　　销: 全国新华书店
开　　本: 185mm×260mm　　　印　张: 9.5　　　字　数: 214千字
版　　次: 2019年6月第1版　　　印　次: 2022年3月第6次印刷
定　　价: 35.00元

产品编号: 082326-01

前 言

随着国际经济贸易的发展和资本的国际流通，经济全球化已经日益深化。会计学科作为企业经济管理的重要工具，与国际接轨显得尤为重要。社会主义市场经济的到来使得我国在对外贸易、国际融资、跨境投资等领域飞速发展，培养新型的会计国际化人才已经成为财经类高校的一项重要任务。

本书以国际会计准则和美国会计准则为导向，其中包括基础会计的基本理论和中级财务会计的进阶会计知识，同时还包含了审计学科的基本内容。通过学习实务中英文的习惯表达和掌握丰富的会计英语词汇，可以帮助学生提高阅读英文会计文献和使用英语处理常规会计业务的能力，满足学生毕业后胜任工作岗位的实际需要。

本书的创新之处在于每章节后配有中英文对照的词汇表，帮助学生自主学习，减少全英文教材阅读给学生带来的理解困难；同时书后配有扩展阅读，介绍了各章的基本理论，英语水平较为薄弱的同学可以通过扩展阅读把握每一章内容的精髓，非会计专业的学生也可以通过扩展阅读了解会计的基本理论、重点和难点。另外，扩展阅读的亮点在于将中外会计准则的差异进行了对比，使学生明确相关会计问题在不同准则下的处理差异。此外，各章节的文末均配有思考题或计算题，帮助学生练习并巩固相关知识点。

《会计英语》按会计学专业主干课程的架构共设11章，其主要内容包括：会计概述；交易事项；应收账款；存货与销货成本；投资；有形资产与无形资产；财务报表；流动负债与长期负债；所有者权益；收入与费用；审计。各章由基本知识、核心词汇、拓展阅读和练习题组成。

本书由景刚副教授、张淼老师担任主编，李佳钰、王文杰担任副主编。参与编写的人员有：景刚、张淼、李佳钰、王文杰、贺琼、闵雪、王昱睿、王梓菡。具体分工如下：景刚负责全书写作大纲的拟定和编写的组织工作；景刚、张淼负责编写第1～5章；李佳钰、王文杰、贺琼、闵雪、王昱睿、王梓菡负责编写第6～11章。为了进一步提升本书的质量，东北财经大学会计学院傅荣教授作为教材主审，并将其多年来对国内外企业会计准则的研究成果融入教材的内容体系中。英国外教Elms Richard Philip老师为本书英文校对做了大量工作，在此一并表示衷心感谢。

在本书的编写过程中，得到了学校领导和相关部门、老师的大力支持与帮助，对此表示衷心的感谢！由于时间仓促，水平有限，本书难免存在疏漏与不足，恳请专家和读者进行批评指正。

编　者
2019年2月

目录

Chapter 1　Fundamentals of Accounting ··········· 1
 Spotlight ··········· 2
 Text ··········· 2
  1.1　Forms of Enterprise Organization ··········· 2
  1.2　Two Kinds of Accounting ··········· 3
  1.3　Accounting Concepts and Principles ··········· 4
  1.4　Elements of the Financial Statements ··········· 5
  1.5　Accounting Equation ··········· 6
  1.6　Accrual Basis and Cash Basis ··········· 6
 Core Words ··········· 7
 Extended Reading ··········· 7
 Exercises ··········· 9

Chapter 2　Transaction ··········· 13
 Spotlight ··········· 14
 Text ··········· 14
  2.1　Transaction ··········· 14
  2.2　Accounting Elements ··········· 15
  2.3　Journal Entry ··········· 17
  2.4　Accrual Accounting ··········· 18
  2.5　Posting ··········· 20
  2.6　Trail Balance ··········· 22
  2.7　Close the Books ··········· 23
 Core Words ··········· 25
 Extended Reading ··········· 27
 Exercises ··········· 27

会计英语

Chapter 3 Receivables	31
Spotlight	32
Text	32
3.1 Variety of Receivables	32
3.2 Account for Uncollectible Account	33
3.3 Measurement of Uncollectible Account	34
3.4 Notes Receivable	35
Core Words	37
Extended Reading	37
Exercises	38

Chapter 4 Inventory and Cost of Goods Sold	41
Spotlight	42
Text	42
4.1 Classifications of Inventory	42
4.2 Inventory and Cost of Goods Sold	42
4.3 Gross Profit	43
4.4 Accounting for Inventory	43
4.5 Various Inventory Costing Method	44
4.6 Summary of Inventory	46
4.7 Lower-of-Cost-or-Market Rule (LCM)	47
Core Words	47
Extended Reading	48
Exercises	49

Chapter 5 Investment	53
Spotlight	54
Text	55
5.1 Short-term Investments and Long-term Investments	55
5.2 Account for Trading Investment	55
5.3 Account for Available-for-sale Investment	57
Core Words	59
Extended Reading	60
Exercises	61

Chapter 6　Tangible Assets and Intangible Assets　63
　　Spotlight　64
　　Text　65
　　　　6.1　Long-lived Assets　65
　　　　6.2　Acquisition Cost of Tangible Assets　65
　　　　6.3　Capitalized Expenditures and Expensed Expenditures　66
　　　　6.4　Account for Depreciation of Plant Asset　66
　　　　6.5　Depreciation Method　67
　　　　6.6　Intangible Assets　69
　　Core Words　72
　　Extended Reading　73
　　Exercises　73

Chapter 7　Liabilities　77
　　Spotlight　78
　　Text　79
　　　　7.1　Current Liabilities　79
　　　　7.2　Long-term Liabilities　82
　　　　7.3　Other Liabilities　87
　　Core Words　88
　　Extended Reading　89
　　Exercises　90

Chapter 8　Stockholders' Equity　95
　　Spotlight　96
　　Text　97
　　　　8.1　Background on Stockholders' Equity　97
　　　　8.2　Classes of Stock　99
　　　　8.3　Issuing Stock　100
　　　　8.4　Cash Dividends　101
　　　　8.5　Stock dividends　101
　　Core Words　103
　　Extended Reading　104
　　Exercises　106

Chapter 9　Revenues and Expenses ... 109

- Spotlight ... 110
- Text ... 111
  - 9.1　Accrual Basis and Cash Basis ... 111
  - 9.2　Measurement of Sales Revenue ... 111
  - 9.3　Merchandise Returns and Allowances ... 112
  - 9.4　Cash and Trade Discounts ... 113
  - 9.5　Expenses ... 114
- Core Words ... 116
- Extended Reading ... 116
- Exercises ... 117

Chapter 10　Financial Statement ... 121

- Spotlight ... 122
- Text ... 122
  - 10.1　Overview of a Financial Statement ... 122
  - 10.2　Formats for Financial Statements ... 123
- Core Words ... 128
- Extended Reading ... 128
- Exercises ... 129

Chapter 11　Auditing ... 131

- Spotlight ... 132
- Text ... 133
  - 11.1　Audit Framework ... 133
  - 11.2　Professional Ethics and Codes of Conduct ... 135
  - 11.3　Standards of Reporting ... 137
- Core Words ... 139
- Extended Reading ... 140
- Exercises ... 141

Chapter 1

Fundamentals of Accounting

Spotlight

Accounting is the important basic work for modern enterprises. It focuses on providing useful information to help make decisions through a series of accounting procedures. The quality of the basic accounting work directly affects the judgment of the information users on situation inside and outside the enterprise. Enterprise managers can forecast and analyze the business status of enterprise through financial information, and evaluate and control all the economic activities of the enterprise. They can also analyze the planning of the enterprise, so that the enterprise can seize the opportunities and avoid risk.

This chapter begins with the basic theory of accounting, and introduces the types of accounting, the basic assumptions of accounting, the accounting elements and accounting equations. It is important to note that all forms of corporate organization require accounting.

Text

1.1 Forms of Enterprise Organization

1.1.1 Proprietorship

A **proprietorship** can also be called a **sole trader**. It is a business with only one owner. Proprietorships shall bear unlimited joint and several liabilities. They tend to be small retail establishments and individual professional businesses such as those of dentists, small restaurants, physicians and attorneys.

1.1.2 Partnership

A **partnership** has two or more persons as co-owners. It is a cooperative relationship between people or groups who agree to share responsibility for achieving some specific goals. Usually, a partnership also bears unlimited joint and several liabilities. The simplest kind of partnership would be that several of you got together and formed a business.

A professional entity that provides paid service to its clients with specialized knowledge and skills may form a specialized general partnership, which can be called a limited liability partnership. In limited liability partnerships, each partner is liable only for his own actions and those under his control. The number of partners can be huge. International accounting firms PwC for example, has over 400 partners in China and the Singapore region.

1.1.3 Limited Liability Company

A **limited liability company(LLC)** is a legal form of a company that provides limited liability to its owners in many jurisdictions. Unlike proprietorship and partnership, the business undertakes limited liability for debts with registered capital instead of individuals. The creditors, such as banks, ordinarily have claims against the corporate assets only, not against the personal assets of the owners.

1.1.4 Public Company

A **public company** is also called a **listed company and corporation**. A public company can offer its shares for sale on the stock exchange. In some jurisdictions, public companies over a certain size must be listed on an exchange. A public company also undertakes limited liability for debts with registered capital. China does not allow unlimited liability companies to exist.

The differences of organization forms are shown in Table 1-1.

Table 1-1 The differences of organization forms

Item	Proprietorship	Partnership	LLC	Public Company
Owner	One owner	Two or more owners	Members	Stockholders
Personal liability of owner for business debts	Personally liable	Personally liable	Not personally liable	Not personally liable

1.2 Two Kinds of Accounting

1.2.1 Management Accounting

Management accounting is also called managerial accounting. It is concerned with the provisions and use of accounting information to managers within organizations (internal users), such as top executives, to provide them with the basis to make informed business decisions that will allow them to be better equipped in their management and control functions.

1.2.2 Financial Accounting

Financial accounting is the field of accounting concerned with the summary, analysis and reporting of financial transactions pertaining to a business. It serves external decision makers (external users), such as stockholders, creditors, suppliers, banks and government.

1.3 Accounting Concepts and Principles

1.3.1 The Entity Concept

The entity concept requires that the transactions of each entity are accounted for separately from the transactions of all other organizations and people. It is the most basic accounting concept. The accounting entity concept is applied to all organization forms of business: single proprietorship, partnership, and corporation.

1.3.2 The Going-concern Concept

The going-concern concept is the assumption that ordinarily an entity persists indefinitely. In other words, an entity will remain in operation long enough to use existing assets for their intended purpose. Under this assumption, an entity reports its long-term assets, such as plant and equipment, based on their historical cost rather than the liquidation value.

1.3.3 The Time-period Concept

For accounting information to be useful, it must be made available at regular intervals. **The time-period concept** ensures that accounting information is reported at regular intervals. The basic accounting period is one year, for example, an entity prepares annual financial reports. An entity also prepares financial statements for interim periods, such as a month, a quarter, and a semiannual period.

1.3.4 The Cost Principle

The cost principle states that assets should be recorded at their historical cost, which is more reliable. In addition to the historical cost, there are other measurement methods, for example, fair value, present value, replacement cost, and net realizable value.

1.3.5 The Stable-monetary-unit Concept

In China, we record transactions in RMB while Americans record transactions in US dollar. The value of RMB changes all the time. A rise in the general price level is called inflation. A decline in the general price level is called deflation. Under **the stable-monetary-unit concept**, we ignore inflation and deflation. Accountants assume that the currency value is stable.

1.4 Elements of the Financial Statements

1.4.1 Financial Position

1. Asset

According to FASB, "an asset is a probable future economic benefit obtained or controlled by an entity as a result of a past transaction or event". That means an **asset** is an economic resource controlled by the entity as a result of past events, which is expected to produce a future benefit, for example, cash, land, plant and inventory. A coffee shop can identify the coffee machine as an asset, since coffee produced by coffee machine can be sold for money.

2. Liability

According to FASB, "a liability is a probable future sacrifice of economic benefits arising from present obligations of an entity to transfer assets or provide services as a result of a past event or transaction." That means a **liability** is a present obligation of the entity arising from past events, which will result in an outflow of resource from the entity. They are debts that are payable to creditors. For example, a bank loan can be identified as a liability, since an entity needs to pay off the principle and interest within a certain time period.

3. Owner's equity

Equity means ownership. In accounting, equity is the residual value or interest of the most junior class of investors in assets, after all liabilities are paid. If liability exceeds asset, a negative equity exists. It is a residual value, which is equal to assets minus liabilities. There are two main sub-parts in **owner's equity**: paid in capital and retained earnings.

1.4.2 Business Performance

1. Revenue

An entity creates **revenue** by providing goods and services to customers. In many countries, revenue is referred to as turnover. In accounting, revenue is often referred to as the "top line" due to its position on the income statement at the very top. This is to be contrasted with the "bottom line" which denotes net income. Revenues will increase the net income as well as the owner's equity of an entity.

2. Expense

In common usage, an **expense** is an outflow of money to another person or group to pay for an item or service, or for a category of costs. For a tenant, rent is an expense. For students, tuition fees are an expense. Buying food, clothing, furniture is often referred to as an expense.

In accounting, an expense has a very specific meaning. It is an outflow of cash or other valuable assets from a person or a company to another person or company. According to International Accounting Standards Board, an expense is defined as "decreases in economic benefits during the accounting period in the form of outflows or depletion of assets or incurrence of liabilities that result in decreases in equity, other than those relating to distributions to equity participants". Expenses are decreases in economic benefits during the accounting period in the form of outflow of assets. Expenses will decrease the net income as well as the owner's equity of an entity.

3. Income

Income is also called profit or earnings. It is the excess of revenues over expenses. When the expenses are more than revenues, an entity recognizes loss.

1.5 The Accounting Equation

The accounting equation states that assets equal liabilities plus owners' equity. This equation will always hold as long as no error has been made. This equation is the basis of double-entry bookkeeping system, and the basis of the statement of financial position. The accounting equations are shown in Table 1-2.

Table 1-2 Accounting equations

Assets = Liabilities + Owners' equity
Assets = Liabilities + Paid in capital + Retained earnings
Income = Revenues − Expenses

1.6 Accrual Basis and Cash Basis

1.6.1 Accrual Basis

Accrual basis is an accounting method that recognizes the impact of transactions on the financial statements in the time periods when revenues and expenses occur.

1.6.2 Cash Basis

Cash basis is an accounting method that recognizes the impact of transactions on the financial statements only when a company receives or pays cash.

Core Words

Proprietorship	个人独资企业
Partnership	合伙制企业
Limited liability company	有限责任公司
Public company	上市公司
Management accounting	管理会计
Financial accounting	财务会计
The entity concept	会计主体假设
The going-concern concept	持续经营假设
The time-period concept	会计分期假设
The cost principle	成本原则
The stable-monetary-unit concept	币值稳定假设
Asset	资产
Liability	负债
Owner's equity	所有者权益
Revenue	收入
Expense	费用
Income	利润
The accounting equation	会计等式
Accrual basis	权责发生制
Cash basis	收付实现制

Extended Reading

1. 资产

资产是指由过去的交易或者事项形成的、由企业拥有或者控制的、预期会给企业带来经济利益的资源。

2. 负债

负债是指由过去的交易或事项所形成的、预期会导致经济利益流出企业的现时义务。

3. 所有者权益

所有者权益也称股东权益,是指企业资产扣除负债后由所有者享有的剩余权益。它在数值上等于企业全部资产减去全部负债后的余额。其实质是企业从投资者手中所吸收的投入资本及其增值,同时也是企业进行经济活动的"本钱"。

4. 收入

收入是指企业在日常活动中形成的、会导致所有者权益增加的、与所有者投入资本无关的经济利益总流入。

按照中国的会计准则,收入按照业务比重进行确认,主要包括主营业务收入、其他业务收入和投资收益等。而本书基于国际会计准则,收入多按照企业业务类型进行分类,分为服务收入(service revenue)、销售收入(sales revenue)、租金收入(rent revenue)等。具体业务处理会在后续章节讲解。

5. 费用

费用是指企业在日常活动中发生的、会导致所有者权益减少的、与向所有者分配利润无关的经济利益的总流出。在我国会计准则中,习惯将成本和费用分开核算,成本与收入一样,按照业务所占比重可分为主营业务成本和其他业务成本;而国际会计准则习惯不区分,直接使用已销商品成本(cost of goods sold)来进行核算。对于期间费用,我国习惯按照费用的用途分为销售费用、管理费用、财务费用,但国际会计准则没有这种分类,而是采用更为细化的会计科目, 如广告费(advertising expense)、人工费(salary expense)、房租费(rent expense)等。

6. 利润

会计利润是指企业的总收益减去所有的显性成本或者会计成本以后的余额。会计利润是根据会计准则计算的结果。计算的基本方法是,按照实现原则确定在一定期间内的收入,按照配比原则确定在同一期间的费用成本,将收入与相关的费用成本相减,即为企业在这一会计期间的利润。为了便于使用者对企业经营情况和盈利能力进行比较和分析，利润表中按多步式对当期的收入、费用、支出项目按性质加以归类，按利润形成的主要环节列示一些中间性利润指标，如营业利润、利润总额、净利润。

Exercises

1. Which enterprise organization has only one owner? (   )
   A. Sole trader.   C. Limited liability company.
   B. Partnership.   D. Listed company.

2. The final result of which kind of accounting is the financial statement? (   )
   A. Management accounting.   C. Auditing.
   B. Financial accounting.   D. Cashier.

3. Why does a going-concern concept exist? (   )
   A. Because the business will not go bankrupt.
   B. Because we can't predict the risk of a corporate.
   C. Because the accounting methods of bankruptcy liquidation are different.
   D. Because it is the most basic accounting principle.

4. Which costing method is the most reliable? (   )
   A. Historical cost.   C. Replacement cost.
   B. Fair value.   D. Present value.

5. Which one is not the interim period of financial statement? (   )
   A. Annual report.   C. Quarter report.
   B. Semiannual report.   D. Month report.

6. Which of the following is the nature of asset? (   )
   A. Asset is controlled by an entity.
   B. Asset can bring the entity future benefit.
   C. An asset is a probable future economic benefit obtained or controlled by an entity as a result of a past transaction or event.
   D. Asset is something owned by an entity due to a past event.

7. If the entity has $10,000 in asset, and $3,000 in liability, how much is the owner's equity? (   )
   A. $3,000.   C. $7,000.

B. $10,000. D. $13,000.

8. If the entity has $10,000 in expense, and $3,000 in revenue, what is the business performance? (   )

A. $13,000 net income. C. $7,000 net income.

B. $13,000 net loss. D. $7,000 net loss.

9. Which accounting subject is affected by net income? (   )

A. Inventory. C. PPE.

B. Cash. D. Retained earnings.

10. When will an entity use cash basis? (   )

A. An entity never uses cash basis. C. When identifies expense.

B. When identifies revenue. D. When making statement of cash flow.

11. What are the differences among proprietorship, partnership, limited liability company, and public company?

12. What are the differences between financial accounting and management accounting?

13. Identify the missing amount for each equation.

Total assets	=	Total liabilities	+	Stockholder's equity
?		180,000		200,000
300,000		100,000		?
250,000		?		140,000

14. Classify the following items as an Asset(A), a Liability(L), or a Stockholder's equity(E).

( )	Account receivable	( )	Account payable
( )	Merchandise inventory	( )	Notes payable
( )	Supplies	( )	Equipment
( )	Common stock	( )	Salary payable
( )	Retained earnings	( )	Dividend
( )	Prepaid expenses	( )	Land

Chapter 2

Transaction

Spotlight

Bookkeeping is also called accounting practice. It is a process of accounting treatment. It usually begins with filling in the certificate and ends with preparation of financial statements. In the time of central planning economy, accounting is only the process of passive implementation of the state regulations. With the continuous improvement of the market economy and continuous innovation of transactions, how to deal with each business more accurately and reasonably is a required technology for many accountants. Thus, bookkeeping is given a particular importance.

Cloris and her friends opened a clinic named Health and Care Clinic. In daily business, a series of economic operations happened. For example, accepting investment, purchasing of fixed assets, purchasing materials, providing service, and paying expense. How to record these items professionally? What is the requirement in the accounting standards when recording these transactions?

Text

In the last chapter, we introduced some basic elements of accounting and accounting equation. This chapter will introduce accounting elements in detail and how to record transactions in journal entry.

2.1 Transaction

A financial **transaction** is an agreement, or communication, carried out between a buyer and a seller to exchange an asset for payment. It involves a change in the status of finance of two or more businesses or individuals. The buyer and seller are separate entities or objects, often involving the exchange of items of value, such as information, goods, service, and money. It is still a transaction if the goods are exchanged at one time, and the money at another. This is known as a two-part transaction: part one is giving the money, part two is receiving the goods. A transaction is any event that has a financial impact on business and can be measured reliably.

There are two elements in the definition of transaction:

(1) As accounting equation is an identical equation, each transaction effects at least two accounting elements.

(2) Financial impact determines what kind of accounting elements to use.

2.2 Accounting Elements

2.2.1 Asset

An asset is a resource controlled by the entity as a result of past and from which future economic benefits are expected to flow to the entity.

Cash means the same as money, especially money which is immediately available. Cash is money in the physical form of currency, such as banknotes and coins. In bookkeeping and finance, cash is current assets comprising of currency or currency equivalents that can be accessed immediately. It is money in the form of paper currency, coins, deposit, and check.

Accounts receivable is a current asset account showing amounts payable to an entity by customers who have made a purchase of goods or service on credit.

Notes receivable is similar to an accounts receivable, but a notes receivable is more binding because the customers signed a note. Notes receivable represent claims for which formal instruments of credit are issued as evidence of debt, such as a promissory note. The credit instrument normally requires the debtor to pay interest and extends for time periods of 30 days or longer. Notes receivable is considered as a current asset if it can be paid within one year, or a non-current asset if it is to be paid after one year. In China, the due time of a note is usually within 6 months.

Inventory is also called merchandise inventory. It is the merchandise that an entity hold on hand which includes raw materials, work in progress goods, and finished goods.

Land account shows the cost of land that an entity uses in its operations, especially when used for farming or building.

Building account shows the cost of purchased office buildings, or manufacturing plants of an entity.

Equipment account shows the cost of tools and machines that an entity need to use in daily production and operation activities, for example, manufacturing equipment and office equipment.

2.2.2 Liability

A liability is a present obligation of the entity arising from a past event, the settlement of which is expected to result in an outflow from the entity of resources embodying economic benefits.

Accounts payable is a current liability account showing the debt from a credit purchase of inventory or service. If it is an account receivable to a seller, then it is an account payable to a buyer.

Notes payable is a note promising to pay a certain amount of money at a certain time, carrying interest. If it is a note receivable to a seller, then it is a note payable to a buyer. It is also used when money is borrowed from the bank.

2.2.3 Stockholders' Equity

Stockholders' equity is also called owners' equity. It is the residual interest in the assets of an entity after deducting all its liabilities.

Common stock account shows the owners' investment in the entity. It can also be used as paid in capital.

Retained **earnings** account shows the cumulative net income earned by an entity, minus its cumulative net losses and dividends over the entity's lifetime.

Dividend is the money declared and paid to the owners by an entity. It is optional, which means the board of directors can decide to pay dividends or not. Dividend is not an expense. It will never affect net income.

2.2.4 Revenue

Revenues are increases in economic benefits during the accounting period in the form of inflows of assets or decrease of liabilities that result in increases in equity, other than those relating to stockholders' investment. The entity uses as many revenue accounts as needed, for example, **sales revenue, service revenue, rent revenue,** and **interest revenue.**

2.2.5 Expense

Expenses are decreases in economic benefits during the accounting period in the form of outflows or depletion of assets or increase of liabilities that result in decreases in equity, other than those relating to distributions to equity participants. An entity needs a separate account for each type of expense, such as **cost of goods sold, salary expense, rent expense, utilities expense,** and **advertising expense.**

2.3 Journal Entry

Cloris Zhang and a few friends opened a clinic near a community, named Health and Care Clinic. During March, 2019, the following transactions happened.

Transaction 1

Cloris and her friends invested $500,000 to Health and Care Clinic, and issued common stock to the stockholders.

Dr: Cash		500,000
Cr: Common stock		500,000

Transaction 2

Health and Care Clinic purchased land for a new location and pays cash of $100,000.

Dr: Land		100,000
Cr: Cash		100,000

Transaction 3

Health and Care Clinic bought some medical supplies in cash, $5,000.

Dr: Supplies		5,000
Cr: Cash		5,000

Transaction 4

Health and Care Clinic earned $4,000 by providing medical service for customers and received cash.

Dr: Cash		4,000
Cr: Service revenue		4,000

Transaction 5

During this month, Health and Care Clinic paid cash for the following expenses: equipment rent, $1,000; employee salary, $3,000; utilities, $500; advertisement fee, $1,000.

Dr: Rent expense		1,000
Salary expense		3,000
Utilities expense		500
Advertising expense		1,000
Cr: Cash		5,500

Transaction 6

Cloris paid $10,000 for a vacation to Australia.

It is a personal transaction, and it is not recorded.

Transaction 7

Health and Care Clinic sold some land which bought in Transaction 2 at its cost.

 Dr: Cash.   100,000

  Cr: Land   100,000

Transaction 8

Health and Care Clinic declared a dividend, and paid cash of $10,000

 Dr: Dividend   10,000

  Cr: Cash   10,000

2.4　Accrual Accounting

In daily operation, an entity doesn't always receive or pay cash when the transaction occurs. According to the accrual basis, we need to adjust this kind of transaction to the proper accounting period.

The purpose of **adjusting**:

- Measure income;
- Update the balance sheet.

2.4.1　Adjusting

Explicit transactions are observable events such as cash receipts and disbursement, credit purchases, and credit sales that trigger nearly all day-to-day routine entries.

Implicit transaction are events that do not generate source documents or visible evidence of the event. We do not recognize such events in the accounting records until the end of an accounting period.

Adjustments are end-of-period entries which assign the financial effects of implicit transactions to the appropriate time period.

2.4.2　Type of Adjusting

1. Deferral

(1) Expiration of **unexpired cost** and **prepaid expense**

Transaction 9

On March 2, Health and Care Clinic purchased $10,000 supplies, and at the end of the month, there were $8,500 supplies left.

Transaction

March 2
  Dr: Supplies   10,000
    Cr: Cash   10,000

March 31
  Dr: Supplies expense   1,500
    Cr: Supplies   1,500

Transaction 10

Health and Care Clinic paid $6,000 for 3 months' rent on March 1.

March 1
  Dr: Prepaid rent expense   6,000
    Cr: Cash   6,000

March 31
  Dr: Rent expense   2,000
    Cr: Prepaid rent expense   2,000

April 30
  Dr: Rent expense   2,000
    Cr: Prepaid rent expense   2,000

May 31
  Dr: Rent expense   2,000
    Cr: Prepaid rent expense   2,000

(2) **Unearned revenue**

Transaction 11

Health and Care Clinic received $9,000 for 3 months' rent on March 1.

March 1
  Dr: Cash   9,000
    Cr: Unearned rent revenue   9,000

March 31
  Dr: Unearned rent revenue   3,000
    Cr: Rent revenue   3,000

April 30
  Dr: Unearned rent revenue   3,000
    Cr: Rent revenue   3,000

May 31

  Dr: Unearned rent revenue   3,000

    Cr: Rent revenue   3,000

2. Accruals

(1) Accrual of **unrecorded expenses**

Transaction 12

Health and Care Clinic borrowed money from the bank, and the interest for March was $750.

Accrual interest

  Dr: Interest expense   750

    Cr: Interest payable   750

Pay interest

  Dr: Interest payable   750

    Cr: Cash   750

Another example is salary payable.

(2) Accrual of **unrecorded revenue**

Transaction 13

Health and Care Clinic lent money to another entity, and the interest for March was $800.

Accrual interest

  Dr: Interest receivable   800

    Cr: Interest revenue   800

Receive interest

  Dr: Cash   800

    Cr: Interest receivable   800

3. Depreciation

Transaction 14

On March 1, 2019, Health and Care Clinic purchased equipment for $12,000. The useful life was 5 years, and the residual value was 0. Suppose Health and Care Clinic used straight-line method.

March 31

  Dr: Depreciation expense   200

    Cr: Accumulated depreciation   200

2.5 Posting

    Accountants use a chronological record of transactions called a journal. But the journal does not indicate how much cash or accounts receivable the entity holds while a T-account can.

For example:

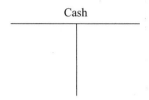

The left side means debit, and the right side means credit.

A **ledger** is a grouping of all the T-accounts.

The process from journal to ledger is called posting.

The ledger of Health and Care Clinic in March is shown in Figure 2-1.

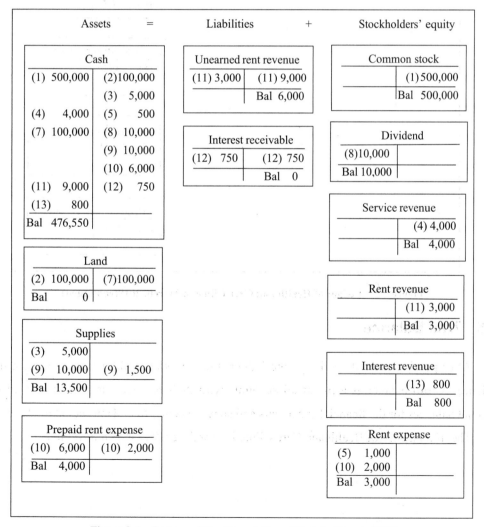

Figure 2-1 Ledger of Health and Care Clinic in March, 2019

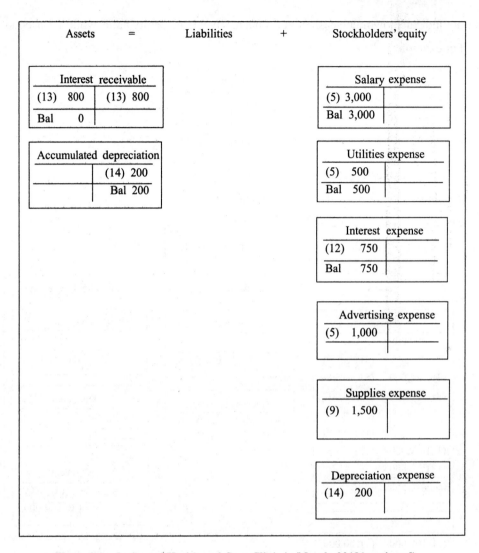

Figure 2-1　Ledger of Health and Care Clinic in March, 2019(continued)

2.6　Trail Balance

After posting journal entries to the ledger, the next step is the preparation of a trail balance. A trail balance is a list of all accounts with their balances. It summarizes all the account balances for the financial statements and shows whether total debits equal total credits.

The trial balance of Health and Care Clinic in March, 2019 is shown in Table 2-1.

Transaction

Table 2-1 Trail balance of Health and Care Clinic in March, 2019

	Trial Balance	
	March 31, 2019	
	Balance	
Account Title	Debit	Credit
Cash	476,550	
Land	0	
Supplies	13,500	
Prepaid rent expense	4,000	
Interest receivable	0	
Accumulated depreciation		200
Unearned rent revenue		6,000
Interest payable		0
Common stock		500,000
Dividend	10,000	
Service revenue		4,000
Rent revenue		3,000
Interest revenue		800
Rent expense	3,000	
Salary expense	3,000	
Advertising expense	1,000	
Utilities expense	500	
Supplies expense	1,500	
Interest expense	750	
Depreciation expense	200	
Total	514,000	514,000

2.7 Close the Books

2.7.1 Temporary Account

Accounts like revenues and expenses, which relate to a limited period are called **temporary account**, for example, revenues, expenses, and dividends.

2.7.2 Permanent Account

Accounts like assets, liabilities, and equities, which carry over to the next period are called **permanent account**. Permanent accounts are not closed at the end of the accounting period.

Close the books means preparing the ledger accounts to record the transactions of next period by making closing entries that summarize all balances in the revenue and expense accounts and transferring the balances to retained earnings.

① *Debit each revenue account for the amount of its credit balance, and credit retained earnings for the sum of revenues.*

Dr: Service revenue	4,000
Rent revenue	3,000
Interest revenue	800
Cr: Retained earnings	7,800

② *Credit each expense account for the amount of its debit balance, and debit retained earnings for the sum of the expenses.*

Dr: Retained earnings	9,950
Cr: Rent expense	3,000
Salary expense	3,000
Advertising expense	1,000
Utilities expense	500
Supplies expense	1,500
Interest expense	750
Depreciation expense	200

③ *Credit the dividends account for the amount of its debit balance, and debit retained earnings.*

Dr: Retained earnings	10,000
Cr: Dividends	10,000

The process of posting temporary accounts is shown in Figure 2-2.

Transaction Chapter 2

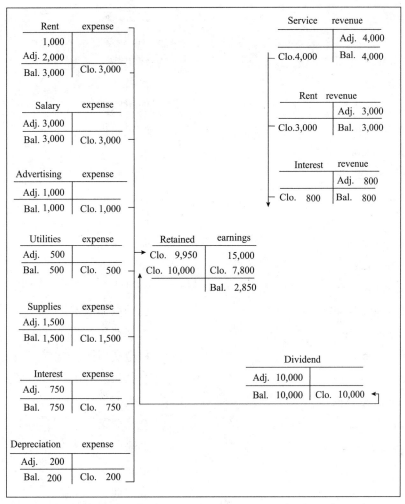

Figure 2-2 Posting temporary account to retained earnings

Why do we need to close the temporary account? Because the balance of a temporary account only relates to one account period.

Core Words

Transaction	交易事项
Cash	现金
Accounts receivable	应收账款
Notes receivable	应收票据

Inventory	存货
Land	土地
Building	建筑物
Equipment	设备
Account payable	应付账款
Note payable	应付票据
Common stock	股本
Retained earnings	留存收益
Dividend	分红
Sales revenue	销售收入
Service revenue	服务收入
Rent revenue	租金收入
Interest revenue	利息收入
Cost of goods sold	已销商品成本
Salary expense	工资费用
Rent expense	租金费用
Utilities expense	公共事业支出
Advertising expense	广告费
Journal entry	会计分录
Adjusting	调账
Explicit transaction	显式业务
Implicit transaction	隐式业务
Unexpired cost	未消耗成本
Prepaid expense	待摊费用
Unearned revenue	预收收入
Unrecorded expense	未入账费用
Unrecorded revenue	未入账收入
Depreciation	折旧
Posting	过账
ledger	账簿
Trail balance	试算平衡
Temporary account	临时账户
Permanent account	长期账户
Close the books	结账

Extended Reading

1. 会计科目表

国际会计准则没有具体的会计科目表，因此，在美国对于会计处理到底采用什么分录没有明确要求，通常是根据业务的明细进行记账。而在我国，则必须使用会计科目表中的会计科目填制记账凭证。

2. 试算平衡

试算平衡，是指在借贷记账法下，利用借贷发生额和期末余额(期初余额)的平衡原理，检查账户记录是否正确的一种方法。本章仅演示了发生额试算平衡，即"全部账户借方发生额合计=全部账户贷方发生额合计"。试算平衡的理论基础就是会计基本恒等式，即"资产=负债+所有者权益"。如果试算不平衡，说明记账工作发生了差错；如果试算平衡，说明记账工作基本正确。但是试算平衡并不能够发现记账过程中的全部错误，如漏记、重记、记账方向颠倒、用错会计科目等情况。

Exercises

1. Which account type usually has a debit balance? (   )

   A. Asset.   C. Owner's equity.

   B. Liability.   D. Revenue.

2. Which account type usually has a credit balance? (   )

   A. Asset.   C. Revenue.

   B. Liability.   D. Both B and C.

3. Which is the most liquid one in current asset? (   )

   A. Cash.   C. Inventory.

   B. Account receivable. D. Short-term investment.

4. Which of the following is a non-current liability? (   )

   A. Account payable.   C. Income tax payable.

B. Salary payable.   D. Long-term debt.

5. Account receivables had a beginning balance of $2,000. During the period, there were debit postings of $1,000, and credit postings of $200. What is the ending balance? (   )

A. $2,800 debit.   C. $1,200 debit.

B. $2,800 credit.   D. $1,200 credit.

6. Account payables had a beginning balance of $2,000. During the period, there were debit postings of $1,000, and credit postings of $200. What is the ending balance? (   )

A. $2,800 debit.   C. $1,200 debit.

B. $2,800 credit.   D. $1,200 credit.

7. Which of the following statements about trail balance is true? (   )

A. If the trail balance is balanced, the accounts must be correct.

B. The trail balance can help to find out all errors in bookkeeping.

C. In trail balance total debits equal total credits.

D. Trail balance is useless.

8. The beginning cash balance is $3,000. At the end of the month, the ending balance is $4,000. If cash paid out during the month is $10,000, what is the amount of cash receipt? (   )

A. $3,000.   C. $11,000.

B. $4,000.   D. $9,000.

9. Purchasing equipment on account will (   ).

A. increase asset.   C. decrease liability.

B. decrease asset.   D. increase expense.

10. Providing service on account will (   ).

A. increase liability.   C. increase asset.

B. decrease liability.   D. decrease asset.

11. AAA Company completed the following transactions during May, 2019.

May	1	Received $60,000 cash , and issued common stock.
	1	Paid $10,000 cash for land to use as a building site.
	1	Paid office rent $450 for this month.
	5	Purchased $800 office supplies on account.
	7	Performed $500 service for customers on account.
	13	Collected $500 from customers on account.
	14	Paid off account payable $800.
	20	Borrowed $10,000 from the bank, and signed a note payable.

(Continued)

	25	Paid the following expenses: salary, $2,000; utilities, $500.
	31	Recognized rent expense for this month.
	31	Paid $1,000 cash dividend to stockholders.

Requirement 1: Record the transactions in the journal.

Requirement 2: Post the journal to the ledger.

Requirement 3: Make trail balance.

Requirement 4: Close the temporary account (journal entry only).

Chapter 3
Receivables

Spotlight

Alice Furniture Manufacturer is a company specializing in furniture production. The factory processes wood to many kinds of fashionable furniture. The company has customers all over the country. However, because of the lengthy transportation times and the shortage of funds from the customers, Alice Furniture Manufacturer can't always receive the money at once. This leads to a large number of receivables from the company. The receivables of Alice Furniture Manufacturer are shown in Table 3-1.

Table 3-1 Receivables of Alice Furniture Manufacturer

Customers	Total Receivables
AAA	$15,000
BBB	$20,000
CCC	$40,000
DDD	$12,000
EEE	$7,000
FFF	$10,000
Total	$104,000

Can all the receivables be recovered? How to deal with the unrecoverable part? Is it possible for an enterprise to estimate the amount which cannot be collected?

Text

3.1 Variety of Receivables

Accounts receivable is a current asset account showing amounts payable to an entity by customers who have made purchases of goods or service on credit.

Notes receivable is similar to accounts receivable, but notes receivable is more binding because the customer signed the note.

(1) By selling goods and service→Accounts receivable

   Dr: Accounts receivable   × × ×

Receivables Chapter 3

  Cr: Sales revenue   ×××

(2) By lending money to others→Notes receivable

 Dr: Notes receivable   ×××

  Cr: Cash   ×××

3.2 Account for Uncollectible Account

  By selling on credit, a company runs the risk of not collecting some receivables. It is called **uncollectible-account expense, doubtful-account expense,** or **bad-debt expense**. How should a company account for these receivables? How do we decide which are collectible and which are not?

  There are two basic ways to record an uncollectible account:

- **Specific write-off method;**
- **Allowance method.**

3.2.1 Specific Write-off Method

  This method of accounting for bad-debt losses assumes all sales are fully collectible until proved otherwise.

  Assume that the ending balance of accounts receivable of Alice Furniture Manufacturer is $100,000 in 2018. In 2019, Alice Furniture Manufacturer collects $97,000 back and the remaining $3,000 is proved uncollectible. The effect of this event on the accounting equation is shown in Table 3-2.

Table 3-2 Impact on the accounting equation

	Asset =	Liability +	Equity
2018	+100,000 Increase in account receivable		+100,000 Increase in sales
2019 write-off	-3,000 Decrease in account receivable		-3,000 Increase in bad debts expense

The journal entry should be:

2019

 Dr: Bad debt expense   3,000

  Cr: Accounts receivable   3,000

The specific write-off method is unreasonable for two reasons:

① Receivables are reported at full amount in 2018, however, the amount of accounts receivable can not be all collected during the year. Therefore assets on the balance sheet of 2018 are overstated.

② The specific write-off method fails to apply the matching principle of accrual accounting. The bad debt of $3,000 should be the result of 2018, however it is recorded as an expense of 2019.

The principal arguments in favor of the specific write-off method are based on the cost-benefit concerns and material. Basically, the method is simple and extremely inexpensive to use. Moreover, no great error in measurement of income or accounts receivable occurs if amount of bad debts are small and similar from one year to the next.

3.2.2 Allowance Method

The best way to measure bad-debts is the allowance method. This method records collection losses based on estimates developed from the company's collection experience. Alice Furniture Manufacturer doesn't need to wait to see whether the customer will pay. Instead, it records the estimated amount as bad-debt expense, and also sets up **allowance for uncollectible accounts, allowance for doubtful accounts,** or **allowance for bad-debts**.

① Sales on account

 Dr: Accounts receivable   100,000

  Cr: Sales revenue   100,000

② Provision for bad-debt

 Dr: Bad-debt expense   3,000

  Cr: Allowance for bad-debt   3,000

③ Write off

 Dr: Allowance for bad-debt   3,000

  Cr: Accounts receivable   3,000

In this way, expenses are confirmed during the reasonable accounting period.

The next problem is the amount of provision for bad-debt expense.

3.3 Measurement of Uncollectible Account

The best way to estimate uncollectibles is using the company's history of collections from customers. There are two basic ways to estimate uncollectibles:

- **Percentage-of-sales method;**
- **Aging-of-receivables method.**

Receivables

3.3.1 Percentage-of-sales Method

Assume that the total sales revenue of Alice Furniture Manufacturer is $40,000 in 2019. Alice Furniture Manufacturer estimates that bad debt expense is 1% of total revenues.

December 31, 2019

    Dr: Bad-debt expense   400

        Cr: Allowance for bad-debt   400

3.3.2 Aging-of-receivables Method

This is an analysis that considers the composition of year end accounts receivable based on the age of the debt. The longer an accounts receivable exists, the higher risk of bad-debt forms.

The receivables of Alice Furniture Manufacturer are classified by age as shown in Table 3-3.

Table 3-3   Receivables of Alice Furniture Manufacturer

Customers	Total	1—30 days	31—60 days	61—90 days	More than 90 days
AAA	$15,000	$10,000		$5,000	
BBB	$20,000	$15,000	$5,000		
CCC	$40,000	$25,000	$15,000		
DDD	$12,000		$10,000		$2,000
EEE	$7,000			$5,000	$2,000
FFF	$10,000	$10,000			
Total	$104,000	$60,000	$30,000	$10,000	$4,000
Historical bad debt percentage		1%	2%	10%	30%
Bad debt allowance	$3,400	$600	$600	$1,000	$1,200

December 31, 2019

    Dr: Bad-debt expense   3,400

        Cr: Allowance for bad-debt   3,400

3.4 Notes Receivable

Notes receivable is more formal compared with accounts receivable.

3.4.1 Key Terms of Notes Receivable

Creditor: The party to whom money is owed. It is usually the bank.

Debtor: A debtor is an entity that owes a debt to another entity. The entity may be an individual, a firm, a government, a company or another legal person.

Principal: The amount of money borrowed by the debtor.

Interest: It is the cost of borrowing money. On a note, it is usually shown as an annual rate.

Maturity date: The date on which the debtor must pay the note.

Maturity value: The sum of principal and interest on the note.

Term: The term is a fixed period of time. It starts from the issuance of a note, and ends when the debtor pays off the note.

A sample of the note is shown in Figure 3-1.

Note

$6,000

March 1, 2019

Bank of China, Dalian Development Zone

On May 31, 2019

Interest at the annual rate of 8%

Michelle Wang

Figure 3-1 Promissory Note

3.4.2 Account for Notes Receivable

March 1
 Dr: Notes receivable   6,000
  Cr: Cash   6,000

March 31
 Dr: Interest receivable   40
  Cr: Interest revenue   40

April 30
 Dr: Interest receivable   40
  Cr: Interest revenue   40

May 31
 Dr: Cash   6,120
  Cr: Notes receivable   6,000
    Interest receivable   80
    Interest revenue   40

Core Words

Accounts receivable	应收账款
Notes receivable	应收票据
Bad-debt expense	坏账费用
Specific write-off method	直接销账法
Allowance method	备抵法
Allowance for bad debts	坏账准备
Percentage-of-sales method	销售额百分比法
Aging-of-receivables method	账龄分析法
Creditor	债权人
Debtor	债务人
Principal	本金
Interest	利息
Maturity date	到期日
Maturity value	到期金额
Term	期限

Extended Reading

1. 应收票据

我国会计准则中，应收票据是指企业持有的未到期或未兑现的商业票据。也就是说，应收票据通常指商业汇票，包括银行承兑汇票和商业承兑汇票两种。而本章介绍的notes receivable和中文的"商业汇票"核算范畴不同，在美国等国家，借钱给第三方企业通常就会签订notes receivable。因此，我们习惯在赊销商品和服务时使用account receivable，由借款产生的应收款项使用notes receivable。

2. 直接销账法

在我国，对于应收账款一律需要按照谨慎性原则，采用计提坏账准备的方法，将坏账费用在合理的期间进行确认。如果不计提坏账准备而采用直接销账法，会导致应收账款产生的会计年度资产被高估，费用被低估，利润被高估；坏账实际产生的年度则资产被低估，费用被高估，利润被低估，不符合权责发生制下配比原则的要求。因此，我国不允许使用直接销账法。国际会计准则中依然还有这种方法存在，但应用也不广泛，仅适用于不常有坏账或者坏账数额较小的企业。

Exercises

1. Which of the following statements is true? (   )

   A. Accounts receivable is more binding than notes receivable.

   B. Accounts receivable is used when lending money to others.

   C. Specific write-off method is better than allowance method.

   D. Uncollectible account is also called doubtful account.

2. Which of the following statements is false? (   )

   A. The best way to measure bad debt is allowance method.

   B. Percentage-of-sales method is better than aging-of-receivable method.

   C. It is better to use the combination of percentage-of-sales method and aging-of-receivable method.

   D. The longer an account receivable exists, the higher risk of bad debt forms.

3. Which one is not the basic element of notes receivable? (   )

   A. Principal.   C. Annual rate.

   B. Maturity date.   D. Address of debtor.

4. Which of the following is the entry for write-off? (   )

   A. Dr: Accounts receivable

   　　Cr: Sales revenue

   B. Dr: Bad debt expense

   　　Cr: Allowance for bad debt

   C. Dr: Allowance for bad debt

   　　Cr: Accounts receivable

   D. Dr: Bad debt expense

   　　Cr: Accounts receivable

Receivables

5. What is the maturity value of a $40,000, 8%, 6 months note? ( )
   A. $1,600.
   B. $3,200.
   C. $41,600.
   D. $43,200.

6. The debit balance of accounts receivable is $1,000. The credit balance of allowance for uncollectible account is $300. If $100 accounts receivable is written off, what is the balance of receivables after write off? ( )
   A. $700.
   B. $600.
   C. $800.
   D. $1,200.

7. The beginning balance of accounts receivable is $15,000. The ending balance of accounts receivable is $18,000. If the total sale of the company during the year is $8,000, how much of the sale is cash sales? ( )
   A. $3,000.
   B. $5,000.
   C. $8,000.
   D. $10,000.

8. Which of the following statements is true? ( )
   A. For an interim statement, companies use percent-of-sales method.
   B. At the end of the accounting period, companies use percent-of-sales method.
   C. Both A and B are right.
   D. Both A and B are wrong.

9. Which of the following statements about credit sales is wrong? ( )
   A. It helps to increase in sales.
   B. The risk of credit sales is an uncollectible expense.
   C. A company can avoid bad debt through internal control.
   D. It is important to pursue collections.

10. The beginning balance of allowance for uncollectible account is $500. The selling amount during the year is $10,000. If the uncollectible account expense is 1% of total sales, what is the ending balance of allowance for the uncollectible account? ( )
    A. $100.
    B. $600.
    C. $400.
    D. $500.

11. AAA Company's balance sheet on December 31, 2018, reported:

Accounts receivable	$420,000,000
Allowance for bad debt	($68,000,000)

AAA Company uses the percentage-of-sales method to estimate bad-debt.

Requirement 1: How much of the December 31, 2018, balance of accounts receivable did AAA Company expect to collect?

Requirement 2: Make journal entries for the following transactions in 2019.
① If the total sale of AAA Company is $500,000,000, and the estimated percentage is 10%.

② Write-offs of uncollectible accounts receivable total $80,000,000. Prepare a T-account for allowance for bad debt with unadjusted balance on December 31, 2019.

③ December 31, 2019, it indicates that $45,000,000 is uncollectible at year end. Post to allowance for bad debt, and show its adjusted balance on December 31, 2019.

Requirement 3: Show the balance sheet on December 31, 2019 related to accounts receivable and allowance for bad debt.

Requirement 4: Show the income statement on December 31, 2019 related to bad debt expense.

Chapter 4

Inventory and Cost of Goods Sold

Spotlight

Danny opened a supermarket named Happy Mall. There are a variety of inventories in the supermarket. The merchandise inventory is Happy Mall's largest asset while the cost of goods sold is the largest expense. How to manage these inventories is the most important issue for the company. However, the cost of the purchase of each batch may be different. The different cost of goods sold may lead to different net income. So how to measure the cost of the inventory sold? How to measure the ending inventory?

The management of inventory has a significant impact on an entity, especially commercial enterprise. Reasonable inventory management can help the enterprise to calculate the profit and report the assets correctly. Through the management of the inventory, the enterprise can achieve the ultimate goal and Improve economic benefit.

Text

4.1 Classifications of Inventory

Inventories are also called merchandise inventories. Inventories can include any of the followings:
- Finished goods product;
- Work in progress being produced;
- Materials;
- Purchased goods.

Inventoy refers to the goods and materials that a business holds for the ultimate purpose of resale.

Cost of goods sold refers to the carrying value of goods sold during a particular period.

4.2 Inventory and Cost of Goods Sold

The connections and differences between inventory and cost of goods sold is shown in Table 4-1.

Table 4-1 Inventory and cost of goods sold

Financial statement	Account	Status
Balance sheet	Inventory	On hand
Income statement	Cost of goods sold	Sold

4.3 Gross Profit

For merchandising firms, an initial step in assessing profitability is calculating gross profit. **Gross profit** is also called gross margin. It is the excess of sales revenue over cost of goods sold. It is the difference between sales revenues and cost of goods sold.

$$\text{Gross profit} = \text{Sales revenue} - \text{Cost of goods sold}$$

4.4 Accounting for Inventory

There are two main types of inventory accounting systems:
- Periodic inventory system;
- Perpetual inventory system.

4.4.1 Periodic Inventory System

This is the system in which the cost of goods sold is computed periodically by relying solely on physical counts without keeping day-to-day records of units sold or in hand.

The periodic inventory system does not involve a day-to-day record of inventories or of the cost of goods sold. Instead, we compute the cost of goods sold and an updated inventory balance only at the end of an accounting period by taking a physical count of inventory.

$$\text{Beginning balance} + \text{New purchases} - \text{Cost of goods sold} = \text{Ending balance}$$
$$\text{Cost of goods sold} = \text{Beginning balance} + \text{New purchases} - \text{Ending balance}$$

4.4.2 Perpetual Inventory System

It is a system that keeps a running, continuous record that tracks inventories and the cost of goods sold on a day-to-day basis. The daily record helps managers control inventory levels and prepare interim financial statements. In addition to this continuous record—keeping process, companies periodically physically count and value the inventory.

No matter which method a company chooses to manage its inventory, it should conduct a physical count at least once a year to check on the accuracy of the continuous record.

Journal entry:

① Inventory is purchased

 Dr: Inventory   ×××

  Cr: Cash   ×××

② Inventory is sold

 Dr: Cash   ×××

  Cr: Sales revenue   ×××

 Dr: Cost of goods sold   ×××

  Cr: Inventory   ×××

The connections and differences between periodic inventory system and perpetual inventory system are shown in Table 4-2.

Table 4-2　Summary of two inventory accounting system

Periodic inventory system	Perpetual inventory system
Used for inexpensive goods	Used for all types of goods
Does not keep a running record of all goods bought, sold, and on hand	Keep a running record of all goods bought, sold, and on hand
Inventory counted at least once a year	Inventory counted at least once a year

4.5　Various Inventory Costing Method

There is a challenge to recognize the cost of goods sold, because the unit price is different every time during purchase inventory. The inventory record of Happy Mall Supermarket is shown in Table 4-3.

Table 4-3　The inventory record of Happy Mall

Inventory			
Beginning balance	20 units@ $20	$400	
Purchase 1	25 units@ $22	$550	Cost of goods sold 55 units@?
Purchase 2	25 units@ $25	$625	
Ending balance	15 units@?		

There are four accepted inventory methods:

- Specific identification method;
- Average cost method;
- First-in, first-out;
- Last-in, first-out.

4.5.1 Specific Identification Method

Specific identification method is also called the specific-unit-cost method. This method concentrates on physically linking the particular items sold with the cost of goods sold that we report. Businesses cost their inventories at the specific cost of the particular unit. This method is relatively easy to use for expensive, low volume merchandise, such as diamond jewelry, vehicles, and houses. This method is too expensive to use for inventory items that have common characteristics.

4.5.2 Average Cost Method

The average cost method is also called the **weighted-average method.** It computes a unit cost by dividing the total acquisition cost of all items available for sale by the number of units available for sale.

$$\text{Weighted average} = \frac{\text{Cost of goods available for sale}}{\text{Units available for sale}}$$

Let's take Table 4-3 as an example:

Cost of goods available for sale=20×20+25×22+25×25=$1,575

Units available for sale=20+25+25=70units

Weighted average cost=1,575÷70=$22.5

Cost of goods sold=22.5×55=$1,237.5

Ending balance=1,575−1,237.5=$337.5

The cost of goods sold and inventory ending balance of Happy Mall is shown in Table 4-4.

Table 4-4 Happy Mall inventory account under average cost method

	Inventory		
Beginning balance	20 units@ $20	$400	
Purchase 1	25 units@ $22	$550	Cost of goods sold 55 units@22.5 =1,237.5
Purchase 2	25 units@ $25	$625	
Ending balance	15 units@ $22.5	$337.5	

4.5.3 First-in, First-out

First-in, first-out is also called the FIFO cost method. This method of accounting for inventory assigns the cost of the earliest acquired units to cost of goods sold.

Let's take Table 4-3 as an example:

Cost of goods sold=20×20+25×22+10×25=$1,200

Ending balance=1,575−1,200=$375

The cost of goods sold and inventory ending balance of Happy Mall is shown is Table 4-5.

Table 4-5 Happy Mall inventory account under FIFO

Inventory					
Beginning balance	20 units@ $20	$400	20 units@ $20	400	
Purchase 1	25 units@ $22	$550	25 units@ $22	550	$1,200
Purchase 2	25 units@ $25	$625	10 units@ $25	250	
Ending balance	15 units@ $25	$375			

4.5.4 Last-in, First-out

Last-in, first-out is also called the LIFO cost method. This method of accounting for inventory assigns the most recent costs to cost of goods sold.

Let's take Table 4-3 as an example:

Cost of goods sold=25×25+25×22+5×20=$1,275

Ending balance=1,575−1,275=$300

The cost of goods sold and inventory ending balance of Happy Mall is shown in Table 4-6.

Table 4-6 Happy Mall inventory account under LIFO

Inventory					
Beginning balance	20 units@ $20	$400	25 units@ $25	625	
Purchase 1	25 units@ $22	$550	25 units@ $22	550	$1,275
Purchase 2	25 units@ $25	$625	5 units@ $20	100	
Ending balance	15 units@ $20	$300			

4.6 Summary of Inventory

The summary of inventory system and inventory costing method is shown in table 4-7.

Table 4-7 Summary of inventory

Question	Description	Method
Which inventory system to use?	Can control inventory by visual inspection	Periodic system
	Cannot control inventory by visual inspection	Perpetual system
Which costing method to use?	Unique inventory items	Specific identification method
	Middle range approach for income tax and income	Average cost method
	Most current cost of ending inventory	FIFO
	Maximize income when cost is rising	
	Most current measure of cost of goods sold and net income	LIFO
	Minimize income tax when cost is rising	

4.7 Lower-of-Cost-or-Market Rule (LCM)

Under the requirement of conservatism, enterprises can not overestimate assets or underestimate liabilities. Therefore, as an asset, the inventory can not be overestimated. The accounting standards require that the enterprises adopt the LCM method and make reasonable reporting for the inventory. In this way, we compare the historical cost and the market value of inventories. Whichever is lower, is used as a new inventory value.

If historical cost is lower than market value, there is no adjustment of inventory. If historical cost is higher than market value, the market value is the new ending balance of inventories. The market value here refers to the current replacement cost. An entity should report inventory at its LCM cost in financial statement.

Suppose Happy Mall bought some boxes of mineral water for $1,800 on November 13, 2019. On December 31, 2019, the market value of mineral water changed to $1,900. There is no need to make adjustments regarding the change. The ending balance of inventory is still $1,800 on the balance sheet.

Suppose Happy Mall bought some boxes of mineral water for $1,800 on November 13, 2019. On December 31, 2019, the market value of mineral water changed to $1,700.

<u>November 13, 2019</u>

Dr: Inventory   1,800
 Cr: Cash   1,800

<u>December 31, 2019</u>

Dr: Cost of goods sold   100
 Cr: Inventory   100

* The ending balance of inventory should be changed to $1,700 on the balance sheet.

Core Words

Inventory	存货
Cost of goods sold	已销商品成本
Gross profit	毛利润
Periodic inventory system	实地盘存制
Perpetual inventory system	永续盘存制

Specific identification method	个别确认法
Average cost method	加权平均法
First-in, first-out	先进先出法
Last-in, first-out	后进先出法
Lower-of-cost-or-market rule	成本与市价孰低法

Extended Reading

1. 实地盘存制

实地盘存制又称定期盘存制，是指通过对期末库存存货的实物盘点，确定期末存货和当期销货成本的方法。实地盘存制无须通过账面连续记录得出期末存货，并假定除期末库存以外的存货均已售出，通过这种方法倒挤出销货成本。因此在实地盘存制下，日常经营中因销售而减少的存货不予记录，而只记录增加的存货。实地盘存制的优点是核算工作比较简单，工作量小。缺点是手续不够严密，不能通过账簿随时反映和监督各项财产物资的收、发、结存情况。当仓库管理中有多发少发、物资损毁、盗窃丢失等情况时，在账面上均无反映，而全部隐藏于本期的发出存货当中，往往会使得成本被高估。因此，实地盘存制不利于存货的管理，也不利于监督检查，只适用于数量大、价值低、收发频繁的存货，与永续盘存制相比安全性较差。

目前实地盘存制一般只适用于核算价值低、数量不稳定、损耗大的鲜活商品。

2. 永续盘存制

永续盘存制又叫账面盘存制，根据会计凭证在账簿中连续记录存货的增加和减少，随时根据账簿记录结出账面结存数量。即对存货的日常记录既登记购进数，又登记发出数，通过结账，能随时反映账面结存数的一种存货核算方法。永续盘存制的优点是可以通过存货的明细账记录，随时反映某一存货在一定会计期间内收入、发出和结存的详细情况，有利于加强对存货的管理和控制。同时可以通过盘点和实存数量进行核对，当发生损溢时，可以查明原因，及时纠正，防止库存的积压或不足。缺点是核算工作量较大。

永续盘存制适用于大部分企业。

3. 先进先出法

先进先出法是指以先购入的存货先发出这样一种存货实物流动假设为前提，对发出存货进行计价的一种方法。采用此方法时，收入存货需逐笔登记收入存货的数量、单价和金额；发出存货时，按照先购进先发出的原则逐笔登记存货的发出成本和结存金额。

使用先进先出法计算的期末存货额，比较接近市价。

4. 后进先出法

在美国有将近一半的企业采用后进先出法，因为后进先出可以帮助企业在物价上涨(通货膨胀)期间合理避税。然而，在我国后进先出法是禁止企业使用的，主要原因在于：后进先出法将更早期形成的成本留在企业存货中，将最近形成的价格分配给销售成本，这样由于通货膨胀的原因长期累积会低估企业存货的公允价值，降低各期的当期利润，同时这种方法也会使得企业应交所得税减少。

后进先出法有几个非常明显的缺点：日常核算工作量大；容易发生后进先出法清算；容易引发不经济的购货行为。

Exercises

1. Which of the following statements about the inventory system is wrong? (   )

    A. In perpetual inventory system, we don't need to count the inventory physically.

    B. Perpetual inventory system can be used for all types of goods.

    C. Perpetual inventory system keeps a running record of inventory.

    D. Perpetual inventory system is better than the periodic inventory system.

2. Which item should be added to recognize the cost of purchased inventory? (   )

    A. Fright-in.   C. Purchase allowance.

    B. Purchase return.   D. Purchase discount.

3. Which inventory costing method is not allowed in China? (   )

    A. Specific identification.   C. FIFO.

    B. Average cost.   D. LIFO.

4. Which of the following statements about specific identification is true? (   )

    A. It can lead to maximum of net income.

B. It can lead to highest ending inventory.

C. It is suitable for inventory with high value and low quantity.

D. It is the most common inventory costing method.

5. The beginning inventory is $18,000, and newly purchase is $50,000. The net sales are $60,000. The gross profit rate of the entity is 35%. What is the ending balance of inventory? (   )

  A. $8,000.   C. $29,000.

  B. $39,000.   D. $50,000.

6. Which of the followings can lead to the most current cost of ending inventory? (   )

  A. Specific unit cost.   C. LIFO.

  B. FIFO.   D. Average cost.

7. Which of the followings can lead to the most current measure of cost of goods sold and net income? (   )

  A. Specific unit cost.   C. LIFO.

  B. FIFO.   D. Average cost.

8. Which of the followings can maximize the reported income when market price is rising? (   )

  A. Specific unit cost.   C. LIFO.

  B. FIFO.   D. Average cost.

9. Which of the followings can minimize income tax when market price is rising? (   )

  A. Specific unit cost.   C. LIFO.

  B. FIFO.   D. Average cost.

10. In lower of cost and market principle, "market" means (   ).

  A. original cost.   C. replacement cost.

  B. present value.   D. net realizable value.

11. AAA Company uses periodic inventory to manage inventory. AAA Company's beginning inventory is 100, @$75. On January 2, AAA bought 200 inventory @$80; on January 15, AAA bought 90 inventory @$85; on January 15, AAA bought 240 inventory @$90. The selling price is $135 each, and there are 130 inventories left at the end of the period.

Calculate the cost of goods sold and gross profit using the average cost method, FIFO, and LIFO respectively.

12. BBB Company uses perpetual inventory to manage inventory. BBB Company's inventory is listed as shown in the following exhibit.

Inventory			
Beginning balance	20 units@ $20	$400	
Purchase 1	25 units@ $22	$550	Cost of goods sold 85 units@?
Purchase 2	25 units@ $25	$625	
Purchase 3	30 units@ $30	$900	
Ending balance	15 units@?		

Calculate the cost of goods sold and ending balance of inventory by using the average cost method, FIFO, and LIFO respectively.

Chapter 5
Investment

Spotlight

In general, to invest is to allocate money or sometimes another resource in the expectation of some benefit in the future – for example, investment in durable goods, in real estate by the service industry, in factories for manufacturing, in product development, and in research and development. However, this chapter focuses specifically on investment in financial assets.

In finance, the benefit from investments is called return. The return may consist of capital gains or investment income, including dividends, interest, rental income, etc., or a combination of the two. The projected economic return is the appropriately discounted value of the future returns. The historic return comprises of the actual capital gain (or loss) or income (or both) over a period of time.

Investors generally expect higher returns from riskier investments. Financial assets range from low-risk, low-return investments, such as high-grade government bonds, to those with higher risk and higher expected commensurate reward, such as emerging markets stock investments.

Investors, particularly novices, are often advised to adopt a particular investment strategy and diversify their portfolio. Diversification has the statistical effect of reducing overall risk.

Investment differs from arbitrage, in which profit is generated without investing capital or bearing risk.

An investor may bear a risk of loss of some or all of their capital invested, whereas in saving (such as in a bank deposit) the risk of loss in nominal value is normally remote. (Note that if the currency of a savings account differs from the account holder's home currency, then there is the risk that the exchange rate between the two currencies will move unfavorably, so that the value in the account holder's home currency of the savings account decreases.)

Speculation involves a level of risk which is greater than most investors would generally consider justified by the expected return. An alternative characterization of speculation is its short-term and opportunistic nature.

5.1 Short-term Investments and Long-term Investments

Short-term investments are also called **marketable securities**. They are investments that a company plans to hold for one year or less. They allow the company to invest cash for a short period of time and earn a return until the cash is needed. Short-term investments are the next-most-liquid assets after cash.

The most typical short-term investments are **trading investments**. Trading investments are usually the stock of another company. The purpose of purchasing a trading investment is to hold it for a short time and then sell it for more than its cost.

Investments that are not short-term are listed as **long-term investments**. They are investments that a company plans to hold for more than one year. Long-term investments are less liquid than current assets but more liquid than property, plants, and equipment.

The most typical long-term investments are **available-for-sale investments.** Long-term investments are usually stocks and bonds that the investor expects to hold for more than one year.

5.2 Account for Trading Investment

5.2.1 Purchase

Vanky Corporation bought AAA stock on March 1, 2019, paying $8,500 cash.

March 1, 2019

  Dr: Short-term investment   8,500
    Cr: Cash   8,500

5.2.2 Receive Dividend

On April 30, 2019, Vanky Corporation received a cash dividend of $50 from AAA company.

April 30, 2018

  Dr: Cash   50
    Cr: Dividend revenue   50

5.2.3 Unrealized Gains and Losses

Trading investments are reported on the balance sheet at their current market value, because market value is the amount the investors can receive by selling the investment. At the year end, investors need to adjust the trading investment to its current market value.

If the market value is greater than the cost of the investment, the margin is called **unrealized gain.**

1. Unrealized gain

Gain because the market value is greater than the cost of the investment.

Unrealized gain applies because Vanky Corporation has not sold the investment yet.

Suppose that on December 31, 2019, the market value of the trading investment increase to $9,000.

December 31, 2019

 Dr: Short-term investment   700
  Cr: Unrealized gain on investment   700

If the market value is less than the cost of the investment, the margin is called **unrealized loss**.

2. Unrealized loss

Loss because the market value is less than the cost of the investment.

Unrealized loss applies because Vanky Corporation has not sold the investment yet.

Suppose that on December 31, 2019, the market value of the trading investment decrease to $7,800.

December 31, 2019

 Dr: Unrealized loss on investment   700
  Cr: Short-term investment   700

5.2.4 Sales of Trading Investment

Sales of trading investment will result in realized gains and losses.

If selling price is greater than the investment carrying amount, the margin is called **realized gain**.

If selling price is less than the investment carrying amount, the margin is called **realized loss**.

1. Realized gain

Suppose that Vanky Corporation had bought AAA stock on March 1, 2019, paying $8,500 cash.

On December 31, 2019, the market value of the trading investment increases to $9,000.

On January 31, 2020, Vanky Corporation sells the trading investment for $9,200 cash.

January 31, 2020

Dr: Cash	9,200	
Cr: Gain on sales of investment	200	
Short-term investment	9,000	

2. Realized loss

Suppose that Vanky Corporation buys AAA stock on March 1, 2019, paying $8,500 cash.

On December 31, 2019, the market value of the trading investment increases to $9,000.

On January 31, 2020, Vanky Corporation sells the trading investment for $8,900 cash.

January 31, 2020

Dr: Cash	8,900
Loss on sales of investment	100
Cr: Short-term investment	9,000

5.3　Account for Available-for-sale Investment

Available-for-sale investment is stock investment other than trading investment. They are classified as currents if the business expects to sell them within one year. All other available-for-sale investments are classified as long-term assets.

Available-for-sale investments are accounted for at market value, because the company expects to sell the investment at its market price. Cost is used only as the initial amount for recording the investments. Available-for-sale investments are reported on the balance sheet at current market value.

Let's take stock investment as an example.

5.3.1　Purchase

Suppose Vanky Corporation buys 10,000 shares of AAA stock on March 1, 2019, at the market price of $3.5, paying $35,000 cash.

March 1, 2019

Dr: Long-term investment	35,000
Cr: Cash	35,000

5.3.2 Receive Dividend

On April 30, 2019, Vanky Corporation receives a cash dividend of $0.03 from AAA company.

April 30, 2019
  Dr: Cash   300
    Cr: Dividends revenue   300

5.3.3 Unrealized Gains and Losses

Available-for-sale investments are reported on the balance sheet at their market value. At the year end, we therefore make adjustment for available-for-sale investments from their last carrying amount to current market value.

If the market value is greater than the cost of the investment, the margin is called **unrealized gain**.

1. Unrealized gain

Gain because the market value is greater than the cost of the investment.

Unrealized gain applies because Vanky Corporation has not sold the investment yet.

Suppose that on December 31, 2019, the market value of the available-for-sale investment increases to $4.

December 31, 2019
  Dr: Allowance to adjust investment to market   5,000
    Cr: Unrealized gain on investment   5,000

If the market value is less than the cost of the investment, the margin is called **unrealized loss**.

2. Unrealized loss

Loss because the market value is less than the cost of the investment.

Unrealized loss applies because Vanky Corporation has not sold the investment yet.

Suppose that on December 31, 2019, the market value of the available-for-sale investment decreases to $3.2.

December 31, 2019
  Dr: Unrealized loss on investment   3,000
    Cr: Allowance to adjust investment to market   3,000

5.3.4 Sales of Available-for-sale Investment

Sales of available-for-sale investment will result in realized gains and losses.

Realized gains and losses measure the difference between the amount received from the sale and the cost of the investment.

If selling price is greater than the investment cost, the margin is called **realized gain**.

If selling price is less than the investment cost, the margin is called realized loss.

1. Realized gain

On May 1, 2019, Vanky Corporation sold the available-for-sale investment for $41,000 cash.

May 1, 2019

 Dr: Cash   41,000

  Cr: Gain on sales of investment   6,000

   Long-term investment   35,000

2. Realized loss

On May 1, 2019, Vanky Corporation sold the available-for-sale investment for $33,000 cash.

May 1, 2019

 Dr: Cash   33,000

  Loss on sales of investment   2,000

  Cr: Long-term investment   35,000

Core Words

Short-term investments	短期投资
Trading investments	交易性金融资产
Long-term investments	长期投资
Available-for-sale investments	可供出售金融资产
Unrealized gain	或有利润(未实现收益)
Unrealized loss	或有损失(未实现损失)
Realized gain	实现收益
Realized loss	实现损失
Market value	市场价值

1. 交易性金融资产

交易性金融资产是指企业以赚取差价为目的而持有，准备近期出售的债券投资、股票投资和基金投资。交易性金融资产是2006年增加的会计科目，主要是为了适应股票、债券、基金等市场交易。交易性金融资产科目替代了原来的短期投资科目，二者反映的内容相似但又有所不同。而在美国依然使用短期投资科目对交易性金融资产进行核算。

交易性金融资产具有如下特点：

(1) 企业持有的目的是短期性的，即在初次确认时即确认其持有目的是为了短期获利。此处所指的短期通常不超过一年(包括一年)。

(2) 交易性金融资产具有活跃市场，公允价值能够通过活跃市场获取。

(3) 交易性金融资产持有期间不计提资产减值损失。

(4) 交易性金融资产以公允价值计量，且其变动计入当期损益。

2. 可供出售金融资产

可供出售金融资产通常指企业初始确认时即被指定为可供出售金融资产的非衍生金融工具，以及没有划分为以公允价值计量且其变动计入当期损益的金融资产、持有至到期投资、贷款和应收账款的金融资产。存在活跃市场并有报价的金融资产到底应该划分为哪类金融资产，完全由管理者的意图和金融资产的分类条件决定。在美国会计准则下，持有意图不超过一年的可供出售金融资产可以划分为短期投资，而持有意图超过一年的可供出售金融资产则划分为长期投资。本章中演示的可供出售金融资产属于长期投资。可供出售金融资产又分为可供出售权益工具投资，如股票；可供出售债券工具投资，如债券。本章中演示的是股票，债券部分见负债章节。

中国会计准则规定，可供出售金融资产应当以公允价值计量。值得一提的是，之前中国会计准则规定其公允价值变动计入资本公积，近年来随着中国会计准则修订过程中对国际会计准则的借鉴，现将其公允价值变动计入其他综合收益。

3. 持有至到期投资

持有至到期投资是指到期日固定、回收金额固定或可确定，且企业有明确意图和能力持有至到期的非衍生金融工具。通常情况下，包括企业持有的、在活跃市场上有公开

报价的国债、企业债券、金融债券等。国际会计准则下，对于持有至到期投资的会计处理和应收票据类似，因此在本章节中没有单独列出。值得注意的是，如果持有至到期投资的持有期限比较长，还应该考虑货币的时间价值，通过年金现值系数和复利现值系数进行折现。

Exercises

1. A company bought the stock of B company on March 1, 2019 for $85,000. A company identifies the stock as a trading investment. On December 31, 2019, the stock is valued at $83,000. What is the balance of this trading investment on the balance sheet? (   )

   A. $85,000.
   B. $83,000.
   C. $2,000 realized loss.
   D. $2,000 unrealized loss.

2. A company bought the stock of B company on March 1, 2019 for $85,000. A company identifies the stock as a trading investment. On December 31, 2019, the stock is valued at $83,000. What should appear on the income statement? (   )

   A. $85,000.
   B. $83,000.
   C. $2,000 realized loss.
   D. $2,000 unrealized loss.

3. The purpose of which short-term investment is to hold it for a short time and then sell it for more than its cost? (   )

   A. Trading investment.
   B. Available-for-sale investment.
   C. Held-to-maturity investment.
   D. Stock.

4. Securities bought and held primarily for sale in the near term should be classified as (   ).

   A. trading investment.
   B. available-for-sale investment.
   C. held-to-maturity investment.
   D. stock.

5. Which of the statements about short-term investment is true? (   )

   A. Short-term investment is reported on the balance sheet after cash.
   B. Short-term is the most liquid item of current asset.
   C. Short-term investment refers to stock.
   D. Short-term investment refers to bond.

6. AAA Company bought a trading investment on June 1, 2018 for $8,700. On December 31, 2018, the value of the trading investment increased to $9,500. On March 10, 2019, AAA sold the trading investment for $9,000.

Requirement 1: Make journal entry.

June 1, 2018

December 31, 2018

March 10, 2019

Requirement 2: Post the journal to T-account.

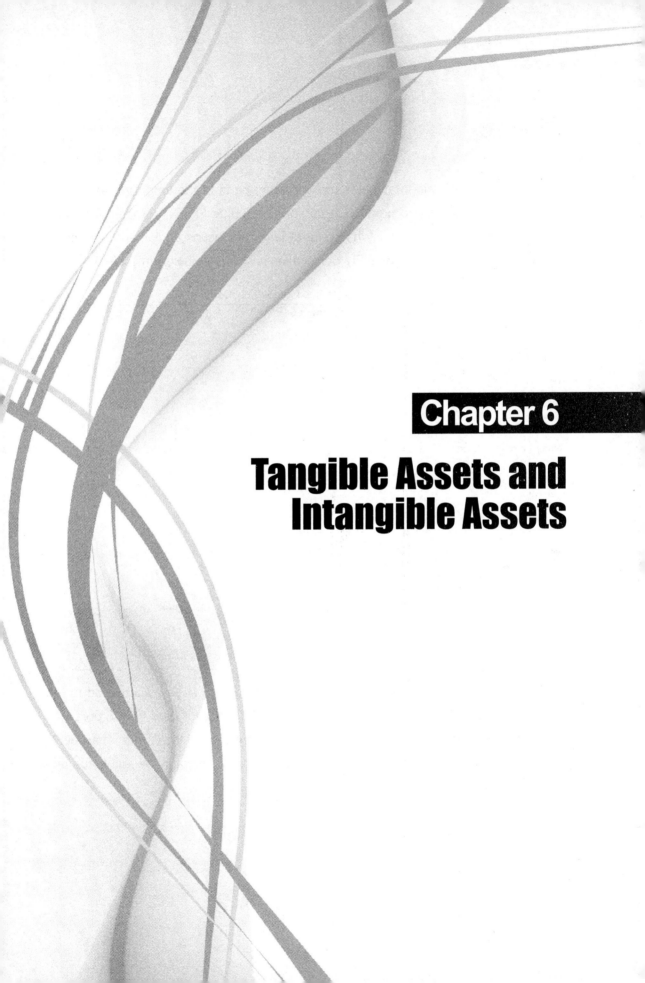

Chapter 6
Tangible Assets and Intangible Assets

Spotlight

Tangible assets and intangibles are important parts of the long-term assets of an enterprise, especially to production corporations. Blue Fly Corporation is a food production factory. This company has a lot of large production equipment and some plants. The balance sheet of Blue Fly Corporation is shown as below in Table 6-1.

Table 6-1 The balance sheet of Blue Fly Corporation

Balance Sheet December 31, 2018	
(*Amounts in thousands*)	
Assets	
Current assets	
Cash and cash equivalents	211
Short-term investments	145
Accounts receivable	245
Inventories	622
Other current assets	<u>43</u>
Total current assets	1,266
Long-term investments	225
Property, plant, and equipment, net	2,288
Intangible assets	399
Other assets	<u>165</u>
Total assets	<u>4,343</u>

Through the report we can find out that the long-term assets accounted for a significant proportion of total assets. It is an important issue for Blue Fly Corporation to manage long-term assets. How to make initial confirmation of the long-term assets? Is the book value of long-term assets invariable? In this chapter, we will focus on accounting for tangible assets and intangible assets.

Text

6.1　Long-lived Assets

Long-lived assets are divided into **tangible** and **intangible** categories. **Tangible assets** are also called **fixed assets** or **plant assets**. They are physical items that people can see and touch, for example, land, buildings, and equipment. In contrast, **intangible assets** are not physical, such as patents, and copyrights.

6.2　Acquisition Cost of Tangible Assets

6.2.1　Land

The acquisition cost of land includes purchase price, survey fees, legal fees, title fees and transfer taxes. It also includes the demolition cost of old structures that must be torn down to get the land ready for its intended use. It doesn't include any cost of land improvement, such as lighting, paving and fencing.

6.2.2　Buildings

1. Constructing building

The cost of a constructing a building includes architectural fees, building permits, constructor charges, interest on money borrowed from bank, and payments for material, labor, and overheads.

2. Purchased building

The cost of purchased building includes purchase price, brokerage commission, taxes, and all expenditures to repair and renovate the building for its intended purpose.

6.2.3　Machinery and Equipment

The cost of equipment includes its purchase price (less any discounts), transportation fees, commission fees, installation cost, and any expenditures incurred for bringing the asset to the expected condition for use.

The acquisition cost of equipment of Blue Fly Corporation is shown in Table 6-2.

Table 6-2 Acquisition cost of equipment

Items	Dollars
Invoice price, gross	200,000
Cash discount, 2%	(4,000)
Invoice price, net	196,000
Transportation cost	2,000
Installation cost	5,000
Repair cost prior to use	2,200
Commissions	4,000
Total acquisition cost	209,200

6.3 Capitalized Expenditures and Expensed Expenditures

When a company spends money on a plant asset, it must decide whether to record it as an asset or an expense.

Costs that increase the asset's capacity or extend its useful life can be called **capital expenditure**, which means the costs are added to an asset account instead of recorded as an expense, for example, an overhaul for a machine.

Costs that do not extend the asset's capacity or its useful life, but just maintain normal use of the asset or restore it to working order, are recorded as **expenses**, for example, a repair cost for a machine.

6.4 Account for Depreciation of Plant Asset

Fixed assets need to be depreciated regularly after they are recorded in the accounts. All kinds of plant assets need to be depreciated, except land. Plant assets are reported on the balance sheet at book value.

Book value=Historical cost - Accumulated depreciation

The journal entry for depreciation is:

Dr: Depreciation expense ×××
    Cr: Accumulated depreciation ×××

Depreciation expense is recorded on the income statement, and accumulated depreciation is recorded on the balance sheet.

6.5 Depreciation Method

How to measure depreciation? There are three elements regarding depreciation.
- Historical cost
- Estimated useful life
- Estimated residual value

Blue Fly Corporation bought a machine for $55,000 on January 1, 2009, the estimated useful life is 10 years or 100,000 working units. The estimated residual value is $5,000.

We introduce three methods of depreciation in this chapter.

6.5.1 Straight-line Depreciation Method

Straight-line depreciation method spreads the depreciable value evenly over the useful life of an asset. Depreciable cost is divided by useful life in years to determine the annual depreciation expense.

$$\text{Depreciation per year} = \frac{\text{Cost} - \text{Residual value}}{\text{Years of useful life}}$$

$$\text{Depreciation per year} = \frac{\$55,000 - \$5,000}{10} = \$5,000$$

The calculations are shown in Table 6-3.

Table 6-3　Blue Fly Corporation: Straight-line depreciation method

Date	Annual depreciation	Accumulated depreciation	Book value
Jan.1, 2009			$55,000
Dec.31, 2009	$5,000	$5,000	50,000
Dec.31, 2010	5,000	10,000	45,000
Dec.31, 2011	5,000	15,000	40,000
Dec.31, 2012	5,000	20,000	35,000
Dec.31, 2013	5,000	25,000	30,000
Dec.31, 2014	5,000	30,000	25,000
Dec.31, 2015	5,000	35,000	20,000
Dec.31, 2016	5,000	40,000	15,000
Dec.31, 2017	5,000	45,000	10,000
Dec.31, 2018	5,000	50,000	5,000(residual value)

6.5.2 Double-Declining-Balance Depreciation Method

Double-declining-balance(DDB)depreciation method is an accelerated depreciation method. There are four steps to calculate the depreciation expense.

(1) Compute the straight-line depreciation rate. The depreciation rate is simply 100% devided by the useful life of an asset.

(2) Multiply the straight-line depreciation rate by 2 to calculate the DDB rate.

(3) Multiply the DDB rate by the book value of an asset.

(4) Determine the final year's depreciation amount.

The calculations are shown in Table 6-4.

Table 6-4 Blue Fly Corporation: Double-declining-balance depreciation method

Date	DDB rate	Annual depreciation	Accumulated depreciation	Book value
Jan.1, 2008	20%			$55,000
Dec.31, 2009	20%	$11,000	$11,000	44,000
Dec.31, 2010	20%	8,800	19,800	35,200
Dec.31, 2011	20%	7,040	26,840	28,160
Dec.31, 2012	20%	5,632	32,472	22,528
Dec.31, 2013	20%	4,506	36,978	18,022
Dec.31, 2014	20%	3,604	40,582	14,418
Dec.31, 2015	20%	2,884	43,466	11,534
Dec.31, 2016	20%	2,307	45,773	9,227
Dec.31, 2017	20%	1,845	47,618	7,382
Dec.31, 2018	20%	2,382*	50,000	5,000

The DDB method is different from the other methods in two aspects:

① Residual value is ignored initially during the first year. Depreciation is computed in full cost of an asset.

② Depreciation expense in the final year is the "plug" amount needed to reduce the asset's book value to the residual amount.

6.5.3 Units-of-Production Depreciation Method

Sometimes the useful life of the asset does not indicate the actual use of the asset, for example, Blue Fly Corporation could depreciate the depreciation of its machine on basis of the actual workload. Suppose the machine's useful life is 100,000 hours.

$$\text{Depreciation per unit} = \frac{\text{Cost} - \text{Residual value}}{\text{Unit of service}}$$

Chapter 6 Tangible Assets and Intangible Assets

$$\text{Depreciation per unit} = \frac{\$55,000 - \$5,000}{100,000} = 0.5 \text{ per working unit}$$

If the machine works 6,000 hours in one year, then the depreciation expenses should be:

$$0.5 \times 6,000 = \$3,000$$

6.6 Intangible Assets

Intangible assets are long-lived assets with no physical form. Intangibles are valuable because they carry special rights from patents, copyrights, trademarks, franchises, and goodwill. Like buildings and equipment, an intangible asset is recorded at its acquisition cost. Intangibles are the most valuable assets of high-tech companies and those that depend on research and development.

6.6.1 Category of the Intangible Assets

1. Patents

Patents are granted by federal government that give the holder the exclusive right for 20 years to produce and sell an invention. The invention may be a product or a process. Like any other asset, a patent may be purchased.

Suppose that Blue Fly Corporation had bought a patent on March 1, 2019 and had paid cash of $100,000. The journal entry for this transaction is :

    Dr: Patent   100,000

        Cr: Cash   100,000

2. Copyrights

Copyrights are exclusive rights to reproduce and sell a book, musical composition, film, software program, and other forms of art. Issued by American federal government, copyrights extend 70 years beyond the owner's life. The cost of obtaining a copyright from the government is low, but a company may pay a large sum to purchase an existing copyright from the owner.

Suppose that Blue Fly Corporation had bought a copyright from a software company on March 1, 2019 and had paid cash of $100,000. The journal entry for this transaction is :

    Dr: Copyright   100,000

        Cr: Cash   100,000

3. Trademarks

Trademarks are also called **brand names**. A trademark is a distinctive identification of a product or service. It is a special name, sign, or word that is marked on a product to show that it is made by a particular company, that cannot be used by any other companies.

A trademark may have a definite useful life set by contract. We should amortize this trademark's cost over its useful life. A trademark or a brand name may also have an indefinite life. Trademarks with indefinite life do not need to be amortized.

4. Franchises

Franchises are privileges granted by a private business or a government to sell a product or service in accordance with specified conditions. It is a permission given by a company to someone who wants to sell its goods or service. The useful lives of many franchises are indefinite, therefore, are not amortized.

5. Goodwill

There are two kinds of goodwill.

(1) Generated goodwill

Generated goodwill is something such as good reputation, which increases the value of the business. Generated goodwill cannot be quantified, so it doesn't belong to the category of accounting.

(2) Consolidated goodwill

Goodwill researched in accounting science is called consolidated goodwill. **Consolidated Goodwill** is defined as the excess of the cost of purchasing another company over the sum of the market values of the acquired company's equity. A purchaser is willing to pay for goodwill when he believes that the company has strong profitability.

Goodwill is only recorded at the time of acquisition. A purchase transaction provides objective evidence of the value of goodwill. Companies never record goodwill that they create for their own business. According to generally accepted accounting principles, goodwill is not amortized because the goodwill of many entities increases in value.

AAA company's financial position is listed as bellow. On January 1, 2019, Blue Fly Corporation had acquired AAA Company, and had paid $120,000 cash. The financial position of AAA company is shown in Table 6-5.

Table 6-5　Financial position of AAA company

December 31, 2018			
Assets		Liabilities	
Cash	$8,000	Accounts payable	$80,000
Supplies	82,000	Long-term debts	15,000
Equipment	52,000	Total liabilities	95,000
Building	40,000		
Total assets	182,000		

Total equity = Total assets − Total liabilities

Total equity = $182,000 − $95,000 = $87,000

The journal entry for this transaction is:

Dr: Cash		8,000
Supplies		82,000
Equipment		52,000
Buildings		40,000
Goodwill		33,000
Cr: Accounts payable		80,000
Long-term debts		15,000
Cash		120,000

6.6.2 Amortization of the Intangible Assets

An intangible asset is recorded at its acquisition cost. The residual value of most intangibles is zero. There are two kinds of intangibles.

(1) Intangibles with **finite lives** that can be measured.

We record amortization for these intangibles. Amortization expense is the title of the expense associated with intangibles. Amortization works like depreciation and it is usually computed on a straight-line basis. Amortization can be credited directly to the asset account as bellow.

Suppose that Blue Fly Corporation had bought a patent on January 1, 2018, and had paid cash of $100,000. On December 31, 2018, the book value should be $95,000. The journal entry for this transaction is :

Dr: Amortization expense	5,000
Cr: Patent	5,000

(2) Intangibles with **indefinite lives**.

We record no amortization for these intangibles. Instead, we check them annually for any loss in value, and record a loss when it occurs. Goodwill is the most typical intangible asset with an indefinite life.

Core Words

Long-lived assets	长期资产(非流动资产)
Tangible assets	有形资产
Fixed assets/Plant assets	固定资产
Intangible assets	无形资产
Land	土地
Buildings	建筑物
Constructing building	自建建筑
Purchased building	外购建筑
Machinery	机械
Equipment	设备
Capitalized expenditures	资本化支出
Expensed expenditures	费用化支出
Depreciation	折旧
Book value	账面价值
Historical cost	历史成本
Accumulated depreciation	累计折旧
Estimated useful life	估计使用寿命
Estimated residual value	估计残值
Straight-line depreciation method	直线法(年限平均法)
Double-declining-balance depreciation method	双倍余额递减法
Units-of-production depreciation method	工作量法
Patents	专利权
Copyrights	版权
Trademarks	商标权
Franchises	特许经营权
Goodwill	商誉
Generated goodwill	自创商誉
Consolidated goodwill	外购商誉
Amortization	摊销
Finite lives	有限使用寿命
Indefinite lives	无限使用寿命

Extended Reading

1. 固定资产

固定资产是指企业为生产产品、提供劳务、出租或者经营管理而持有的，使用时间超过12个月的，价值达到一定标准的非货币性资产，包括房屋、建筑物、机器、机械、运输工具以及其他与生产经营活动有关的设备、器具、工具等。

可选用的折旧方法包括年限平均法、工作量法、双倍余额递减法和年数总和法等。固定资产的折旧方法一经确定，不得随意变更。固定资产应当按月计提折旧，并根据其用途计入相关资产的成本或者当期损益。

值得注意的是，当月增加的固定资产当月不计提折旧，从下月起计提折旧；当月减少的固定资产，当月仍计提折旧，从下月起停止计提折旧。固定资产折足折旧后，不管能否继续使用，均不再提取折旧；提前报废的固定资产，也不再补提折旧。

2. 无形资产

无形资产是指企业拥有或控制的没有实物形态的可辨认非货币性资产，通常包括专利权、非专利技术、商标权、著作权、特许权、版权等。

需要注意的是，我国实行土地公有制，所以土地是以土地使用权的形式作为无形资产入账，而大多数资本主义国家都将土地直接作为固定资产来入账。本章考虑到会计英语实际应用的意义，将土地作为固定资产进行讲解。

根据《中华人民共和国著作权法》的规定，版权所有人可以在法律规定年限内对作品享有独占权。版权的期限对个人而言是作者终生及死亡后50年，而美国相关法律规定的期限则为死亡后70年。

Exercises

1. All of the tangible assets need to be depreciated, except (   ).

A. plant.
B. land.
C. building.
D. equipment.

2. Depreciation is a process of (   ).

A. allocation of cost.
C. appraisal of asset.
B. valuation of asset.
D. none of the above.

3. A company bought a new machine for $80,000 on January 1, 2018. The estimated residual value of the machine is $2,000. The estimated useful life of the machine is 5 years. The company uses straight-line method to make depreciation. What is the amount of accumulated depreciation on December 31, 2019? (   )

A. $15,600.
C. $16,000.
B. $31,200.
D. $32,000.

4. A company bought a new machine for $17,000 on January 1, 2018. The estimated residual value of the machine is $2,000. The estimated useful life of the machine is 4 years. The company uses straight-line method to make depreciation. What is the amount of accumulated depreciation on December 31, 2019? (   )

A. $3,750.
C. $12,750.
B. $7,500.
D. $8,500.

5. Which is the necessary item to calculate depreciation? (   )

A. Historical book value.
C. Estimated residual value.
B. Estimated useful life.
D. All of the above.

6. Which of the following can be identified as a capital expenditure of a car? (   )

A. Overhaul of the car.
C. Change of engine oil.
B. Repair of car paint.
D. Car wash.

7. Which method can be used for amortization of intangible assets? (   )

A. Straight-line method.
C. Double-Declining-Balance method.
B. Units-of-Production Depreciation method.
D. All of the above.

8. Which of the following is not an intangible asset? (   )

A. A patent.
C. Land.
B. A copyright.
D. A trademark.

9. Which of the statements is false? (   )

A. The net book value of a tangible asset equals the cost minus accumulated depreciation.

B. The estimated useful life is the length of service that a business expects to get from an asset.

C. Goodwill is the reputation of a business.

D. Plant assets can also be called fixed assets.

Tangible Assets and Intangible Assets — Chapter 6

10. Which of the statements is true? (   )

A. The cost of a purchased asset includes all the cost required to get the asset ready for its intended use.

B. DDB method is an accelerated depreciation method.

C. The various depreciation techniques are all algorithmic ways of spreading an asset's historical cost over time.

D. All of the above.

11. Suppose that AAA Company had bought a machine for $85,000 on January 1, 2013. The estimated useful life is 6 years. The estimated residual value is $5,000.

Requirement 1: Use straight-line depreciation method to calculate depreciation expense, accumulated depreciation, and book value each year, filling the form below.

Date	Annual depreciation	Accumulated depreciation	Book value
Jan.1, 2013			
Dec.31, 2013			
Dec.31, 2014			
Dec.31, 2015			
Dec.31, 2016			
Dec.31, 2017			
Dec.31, 2018			

Requirement 2: Use DDB depreciation method to calculate depreciation expense, accumulated depreciation, and book value each year, filling the form below.

Date	DDB rate	Annual depreciation	Accumulated depreciation	Book value
Jan.1, 2013				
Dec.31, 2013				
Dec.31, 2014				
Dec.31, 2015				
Dec.31, 2016				
Dec.31, 2017				
Dec.31, 2018				

Chapter 7
Liabilities

Spotlight

The Juicy-juice company started by selling fashionable clothes for young people, and now the company has more than 200 retail stores across China. In times of rapid expansion, the Juicy-juice company had borrowed money from banks and investors to open new stores. The company took out a loan from a bank for $100 million and borrowed 1 billion in the form of bonds in 2018. In this chapter, we learn how the company accounts for the money they borrowed.

Why would the Juicy-juice company want to have so much debt? The reason why most companies borrow money is that the management believes that remaining competitive requires continual growth. In the meantime, the borrowed money can increase the sales and earnings, which can bring more benefits to the management and shareholders.

The liability part of the Juicy-juice company's balance sheet is shown in Table 7-1 as follows.

Table 7-1 The liability part of the Balance Sheet

Juicy-juice company Dec. 31, 2018 (dollars in millions)		
	2018	2017
Current liabilities		
Short-term debt	$-	$150
Current maturities of long-term debt	240	140
Accounts payable	1,200	1,100
Accrued expenses	980	1,000
Income taxes payable	280	260
Total current liabilities	2,700	2,650
Long-term debt		
Long-term note payable	100	900
Long-term bonds payable	1,060	800
Deferred income taxes	770	760
Other liabilities	510	450
Total long-term liabilities	2,440	2,910
Total debt	$5,140	$5,560

Liabilities — Chapter 7

Text

You have learned about the accounting treatment of inventories, plant assets, and investments, Now we will learn how to use current liabilities and long-term liabilities to purchase these assets.

Liabilities refers to the past transactions or matters formed by the enterprise, which is expected to be obligations to pay cash or to provide goods and services to other companies or individuals.

As our accounting process is based on the accrual basis, such liabilities are recognized as they occur, not necessarily when companies pay them by cash.

Liabilities can be classified as **current liabilities** and **long-term liabilities**, and such classification can help financial statement analysis recognize the immediacy of the company's obligations.

Current liabilities are obligations that fall due within the coming year or within the company's normal operating cycle (if that cycle is longer than one year).

The current liabilities include wages due to employees, payables to suppliers, taxes owed the government, and so on.

Long-term liabilities are those that fall due more than one year beyond the balance sheet date.

The long-term liabilities include interest and principal due to lenders, such as the suppliers, banks or the government. Companies usually pay long-term obligations gradually, yearly or monthly.

In the general ledger, companies keep separate accounts for different liabilities, such as wages, commissions, taxes, bonds, interests and some other items. **Table 7-1** lists the liability part of the balance sheet.

We defined different types of **current liabilities** as a result of different transaction entities, such as employees, the government, or a supplier. Let's take a look at the accounting procedures for some different types of current liabilities.

7.1 Current Liabilities

7.1.1 Accounts Payable

Accounts payable are amounts owed to suppliers by purchasing materials, goods or accepting services.

As in common practice, the accounting subject —— **accounts payable** is the largest amount in current liability for most companies. Therefore, you can find **accounts payable** is always set as a separate line item under current liabilities on their balance sheets.

Suppose the Juicy-juice company purchas a number of inventories for $1,000,000 and appoint to make payments next month. The journal entry for this transaction is as follow:

  Dr: Inventory   1,000,000
   Cr: Accounts payable 1,000,000

7.1.2 Notes Payable

Taking loans is a common form of financing. When companies take out a loan from a bank, they have to sign promissory notes, which are showed on financial statements as **notes payable**. However, you should pay attention to whether the **notes payable** is a short-term obligation due within one year. If the obligation to repay the loan principle and interest is over one year, such obligation belongs to the long-term liabilities.

Suppose that the Juicy-juice company had taken a loan from the bank for $1,000,000 on March 1, 2018. The journal entry for this loan is:

  Dr: Cash   1,000,000
   Cr: Notes payable   1,000,000

7.1.3 Accrued Employee Compensation

Accrued liabilities usually result from the expenses the company has incurred but not yet paid. Therefore, the accrued expenses create liabilities, so such expenses are called **accrued expenses**.

One common accrued expense is obligations to employees for their weekly or monthly wages. As the payment of wages, salaries and commissions occur frequently for most companies, such obligations are usually shown on the financial statements as a separate line, called **(accrued) wages payable, (accrued) salary payable or (accrued) commission payable**.

Suppose at the end of June, 2018, the Juicy-juice company still had had $1 million compensation expenses not yet paid to the employees until the next month. The journal entry for this liability is:

Liabilities

```
Dr: Compensation expense              1,000,000
    Cr: Salaries and wages payable        1,000,000
```

7.1.4 Income Taxes Payable

In most countries of the world, companies have obligations to pay taxes to the government to insure the whole society runs well. A typical one is **income tax**, the part of the corporations' earnings. Instead of paying one lump sum at tax time, corporations make periodic installment payments based on their estimated tax for the year. Therefore, the income taxes payable are the amount of income taxes the company still owes at the end of year.

To illustrate, suppose Juicy-juice company had had an estimated pre-tax income of $10 million for the year 2018. At a 40% tax rate, the company's estimated income taxes for the year were $4 million. The company would pay the income taxes as bellow:

	March 15	June 15	September 15	December 15
Estimated income taxes (in millions)	$1	$1	$1	$1

As we know, in most cases the estimated pre-tax income might not be the same as the final exact income at the end of year. Therefore, the company must file a final income tax return and make a final payment by March 15, 2019. Suppose the actual pre-tax income for the year 2018 was $11 million instead of the estimated $10 million. The total income taxes would then be $4.4 million. By the next year's March 15, the company must pay the $0.4 million additional income tax.

The journal entry for this extra $0.4 million income taxes payable is:

```
Dr: income taxes                400,000
    Cr: income taxes payable        400,000
```

For simplicity, the illustration assumed equal quarterly payments. However, the estimated taxable income for a calendar year may change as the year unfolds. The corporation must change its quarterly payments accordingly. Regardless of how a company changes its estimates, there will always be a tax payment or refund due on March 15, and there will be an accrual adjustment at the end of year.

7.1.5 Current Portion of Long-Term Debt

The long-term debt could be paid in several periods, but the **current portion** of **long-term debt** (also called **current maturity** or **current installment**), which is the amount of the principle that is payable within one year, should be reclassified from the long-term liability to the current liability.

Using the Juicy-juice company's example, the journal entry for recognizing the current portion of long-term debt of $23,000,000, the reclassification journal entry for long-term debt that becomes due in fiscal 2018 would be:

  Dr: Long-term debt   23,000,000
    Cr: Current maturities of long-term debt   23,000,000

7.1.6 Unearned Revenue

Unearned revenue is also called **deferred revenues** and **revenues collected in advance**, is revenue for which the business has collected cash from customers before it delivers services or goods. These unearned revenues are current liabilities for the reason that they require a company either to deliver the products or service or to make a full refund.

Let's consider an example: on March 10, 2018, Juicy-juice company collected a customer's pre-paid money in advance for $800, and the clothes would be mailed to the customer the next week. Prepare the journal entry:

  <u>March 10, 2018</u>
    Dr: Cash   800
      Cr: Unearned sales revenues   800
  <u>March 17, 2018</u>
    Dr: Unearned sales revenues   800
      Cr: Sales   800

Airline companies sell tickets and collect cash in advance. Therefore, airline companies usually have large sums of unearned revenues on their balance sheets. Other examples include rental contracts, insurance premiums, purchasing train or theater tickets, magazine subscriptions, and so on.

7.2 Long-term Liabilities

Long-term liabilities are obligations that would be due over one year. Long-term liabilities include two main items: bonds and notes payable. Large companies need financing to collect cash to run their operating and investing activities. Large companies can borrow millions from the bank by signing a promissory note, which becomes **a long-term note payable** on the balance sheet. But they cannot borrow billions from a single lender, so how do corporations collect huge sums? They issue **bonds** to the public which becomes a **bond payable**. How

Liabilities

exactly do lenders and borrowers measure the value of such long-term obligations? They use the time value of money, which means that a dollar you expect to pay or receive in the future is not worth as much as a dollar you have today.

7.2.1 Bonds

Large corporations have heavy demands for borrowed capital, so they often issue corporation **bonds** to the public in the financial markets. Purchasers of bonds receive a bond's formal certificate, which carries the **principle, the payment date** and **interest rates**. The principle is also called the bond's **face value**, **maturity value**, or **par value**. The certificate also states that the issuing company should pay the debt at a specific future time called the **maturity date**.

We regard the interest as the rental fee on borrowed money of the issuing company. The issuing company should pay the interest at a specified annual rate at a fixed interest rate on the bonds certificate. The **interest rate** is also called the **nominal interest rate, contractual rate, coupon rate,** or **stated rate**. Bonds generally pay interest every month or every 6 months.

7.2.2 Types of Bonds

1. Mortgage bonds and subordinated debentures

When a company is in liquidation, the bond provisions determine the bondholders' priority for their claims and the amount the bondholders could get from the liquidating assets and cash. The **mortgage bonds** and **subordinated debentures** have different priority for the claims.

The **mortgage bonds** are secured by the agreed specific property on the covenants, which means these bondholders have the first right to the claims of the specific property in the liquidating process.

In contrast, the **subordinated debenture** holders are not secured by any property in their bond covenants, which means they have a lower priority claim to collect their bond amount. In detail, the subordinated debenture holders have claims against only the remaining assets after other general creditors at liquidation.

2. Callable and convertible bonds

A **callable bond**, or **redeemable bond**, gives the bond issuer the right to purchase the bond back from the bond holders before the maturity date of the bond through an embedded call option. Such issuers will compensate the bond holders with an option premium to allow themselves the opportunity to purchase the bond back if they paid the bond holders a higher coupon than the market bears.

In finance, a **convertible bond** is a type of bond that the holder can convert it into a specified number of shares of common stock in the issuing company or cash of equal value. Because of the conversion superiority, convertible bonds usually have a lower interest rate than similar bonds without the conversion privilege.

7.2.3 Issuing Bonds

There are three ways for corporations to issue bonds: **issuing at par, issuing at premium** and **issuing at discount**. The issuing types are determined by the relative sizes between the **market rate** and **coupon rate**. The market rate is the rate available on investment in similar bonds at a moment in time. It is the interest that investors require if they are tending to purchase the bond. A bond issued at a price equal to its face value is called **issued at par**. In some situations, the bond's market rate differs from the coupon rate. A bond issued at a price higher than its face value is called **issued at premium**, and in contrast, if a bond is issued at a price below its face value it is called **issued at discount**.

1. Issuing bonds payable at par

Suppose that on January 1, 2018, Juicy-juice company issued 1 billion, 2-year, annual 10% interest debentures, at par, which means the market rate is the same the the coupon rate and there is no premium or discount on these bonds payable.

The company has to pay back the principle of $ 1 billion two years later and the company must pay the interest for such bond by every half year. The interest expense equals the amount of the interest payments: 10% × $1 billion × 1/2 = $50 million each 6 months for a total of $200 million over the four semiannual periods. Table 7-2 shows the process how the bonds affect Juicy-juice company's balance sheet equation in its 2-year life, assuming the company does not retire them before maturity.

Table 7-2 The effect of issuing bonds on balance sheet equation

Bond Transactions: Issued at Par ($in millions)				
	A	= L	+	SE
	Cash	Bonds payable		Retained earnings
Issuer's records				
1. Issuance	+1,000 =	+1,000		
2. Semiannual interest (repeated twice a year for 2 years)	-200 =			Increase interest expense -200
3. Maturity value (final payment)	-1,000 =	-1,000		

The journal entries for the issue are:

(1) Dr: Cash　　　　　　　　　　　　1,000, 000, 000
　　　Cr: Bonds payable　　　　　　　　1,000, 000, 000
(2)~(5) Dr: Interest expense　　　　　　50,000, 000
　　　Cr: Cash　　　　　　　　　　　　50,000, 000
(6) Dr: Bonds payable　　　　　　　　1,000, 000, 000
　　　Cr: Cash　　　　　　　　　　　　1,000, 000, 000

Entry (1) is at issue, entries (2) through (5) are the four identical interest payments, and entry (6) is the repayment of principal at maturity.

2. Issuing bonds payable at a discount

On January 1, 2018, the Juicy-juice company issued 1 billion, 2-year, annual 10% interest debentures. The annual market interest rate is 12%, which is a 6% rate for each six-month period. We can recognize that the market rate is higher than the coupon rate, which means that the issuer has to decrease the issuing price, or no investor would choose such bonds with a lower interest rate. However, how can the amount of discount be determined? According to checking the present value table, we get the present value factor as shown in Table 7-3.

Table 7-3　Computation of Market Value of $1 billion principle, 10% coupon, 2-year bond(in millions)

	Present value factor	Total present value
Valuation at market rate of 12% per year, or 6% per half-year		
Principle	0.792,1	792.10
Interest	3.465,1	173.25
Total		965.35

The Juicy-juice company could only collect $965.35 million for issuing such bonds. Therefore, the company recognizes a discount of $ 1,000 − $965.35 = $34.65 million at issuance. The journal entry for the issue should be:

　　Dr: Cash　　　　　　　　　　　　　965,350,000
　　　　Discount on bonds payable　　　　34,650,000
　　　　Cr: Bonds payable　　　　　　　　1,000, 000, 000

When making the bookkeeping of this discount on bonds payable, please note that the discount is a contra account. The bonds payable account on the books usually shows the face value, and deduct the discount amount from the face amount, then we get the amount shown on the balance sheet, often referred to as the net liability:

Issuer's balance sheet	January 1, 2018
Bonds payable, 10% due December 31, 2017	$1,000,000,000
Deduct: Discount on bonds payable	34,650,000
Net liability (book value	$965,350,000

3. Bonds issued at a premium

Again, we suppose that on January 1, 2018, the Juicy-juice company had issued 1 billion, 2-year, annual 10% interest debentures. The annual market interest rate is 8%, which is a 4% rate for each six-month period. Considering this example, the coupon rate exceeds the market rate, which could lead the issuer to a loss on issuing such bonds because the issuer gives a higher interest rate than others in the same market. We still use the present value table to check out the present value factor on 4% with four periods as shown in Table 7-4.

Table 7-4 Computation of market value of $1 billion principle, 10% coupon, 2-year bond

(in millions)

	Present value factor	Total present value
Valuation at market rate of 12% per year, or 6% per half-year		
Principle	0.854,8	854.80
Interest	3.629,9	181.50
Total		1,036.30

As Juicy-juice company issued a higher coupon rate, the bonds are issued at premium to cover the interest loss. The company could receive $1,036.3 million for the bonds. The balance sheets show the net liability calculated as the face amount plus unamortized premium.

(1) Dr: Cash   1,036,300,000
    Cr: Premium on bonds payable   36,300,000
        Bonds payable   1,000,000,000

(2) Dr: Interest expenses   41,451,700
    Premium on bonds payable   8,548,300
    Cr: Cash   50,000,000

(3) Dr: Interest expenses   41,109,800
    Premium on bonds payable   8,890,200
    Cr: Cash   50,000,000

(4) Dr: Interest expenses   4,754,200
    Premium on bonds payable   245,800
    Cr: Cash   50,000,000

(5) Dr: Interest expenses	4,384,300	
Premium on bonds payable	9,615,700	
Cr: Cash		50,000,000
(6) Dr: Bonds payable	1,000,000,000	
Cr: Cash		1,000,000,000

7.3 Other Liabilities

7.3.1 Pensions and Other Post-retirement Benefits

Many companies have retirement plans for their employees. Accountants place these benefits into two categories: **pensions**, which are employee compensations that will be received during retirement, and **other post-retirement benefits**, such as medical insurance for retired former employees.

Pension is one of the most complex accounting areas because the employers contribute money directly into a fund that belongs to the employees. An employee's retirement payments will depend on the amount in the fund at the time he or she retires.

7.3.2 Deferred Taxes

When a company delays the payment of taxes from the time it earns income, this delayed amount could lead to short-term taxes payable. In another situation, because sometimes income tax rules and the accounting principle requirements for financial reporting differ, the difference between reporting and tax laws forces companies to record some income tax expense long before they pay the taxes. Such a situation could create a deferred income tax liability.

7.3.3 Contingent Liabilities

The liabilities you have learned about so far are all concrete, however, the contingent liability is not an accrual liability. In contrast, a contingent liability is a potential liability that depends on the future outcome of a past event. Examples of contingent liabilities are future obligations that may arise because of lawsuits, tax disputes, and so on. If the probability that the event would occur was high and the company can reasonably estimate the amount of the obligation, the company should disclose the substance of their financial positions.

Core Words

Liabilities	负债
Current liability	流动负债
Long-term liability	长期负债
Accounts payable	应付账款
Notes payable	应付票据
Accrued employee compensation	应付职工薪酬
Income taxes payable	应交所得税
Current portion of long-term debt	一年内到期长期负债
Unearned revenue	预收账款
Debenture	债券
Corporate bonds	公司债券
Stated rate	票面利率
Par value	面值
Mortgage bond	担保债券
Subordinated debenture	次级债券
Callable bonds	可赎回债券
Convertible bonds	可转换债券
Market rate	市场利率
Bond discount	债券折价
Bond premium	债券溢价
Callable bonds	可赎回债券
Liquidation	清算
Pension	退休金
Other post-retirement benefits	其他退休后津贴
Deferred income tax liability	递延所得税负债
Contingent liability	或有负债

Extended Reading

1. 流动负债的中外比较

(1) 有关流动负债的概念在外延上及内涵上不尽一致

美国财务会计准则委员会在1980年的第3号财务概念公告中,将流动负债定义为:"将在一年或一个正常的经营周期内,并期望要求应用那些已经适当地划分为流动资产的现有来源,或通过产生其他流动负债来加以清偿的责任。"而我国《企业会计准则》将流动负债定义为:"将在一年内或超过一年的一个营业周期内偿还的债务。"

从两者所下的定义可看出,西方关于流动负债概念的规定有两个特点:一是在内容上,将流动资产与流动负债联系起来,考虑了它们之间有相互联系,从而有助于正确地反映企业的财务状况;二是在时间上,不机械地以"一年"为界,这样就考虑了不同企业的不同经营周期,从而能客观地反映流动负债的"流动"特征。

(2) 有关流动负债的会计处理及界定方法不一致

我国颁布的会计准则规范的负债是指现实存在的,即现实的负债。而西方国家在会计处理上不同,其所指的负债不仅指现实的负债,也包括未来可能发生的负债——或有负债。

2. 可转换债券的中外会计处理差异

所谓可转换债券,是指其持有者可以在一定时期内按一定比例或价格将信用债券转换成一定数量的普通股票的债券。可转换债券既不同于传统股票,也不同于传统债券,而是一种兼债权与股权性质于一身的混合式金融工具。一方面,它具有明显的债务性质,如果投资者在转换期内未将其转换为股票,发行人必须无条件地还本付息;另一方面,可转换债券又具有股权性质,持有人可在规定的时间内按条件将其转换为普通股,在转换之后,由被投资企业的债务转为股本。在规定的转换期内,投资者既可以选择行使转换权,也可以放弃转换权利。正是因为这种混合性,对现存的会计实务提出了挑战,到底是把可转换债券作为债务处理,还是作为权益处理?

(1) 国内的处理方法

我国财政部2006年颁布的新会计准则及指南,对可转换债券等金融衍生工具的会计处理做出了以下规定。

对于发行方，企业发行的某些非衍生金融工具(如可转换公司债券等)既含有负债成分，又含有权益成分，应在初始确认时，将相关负债和权益成分进行拆分，先对负债成分的未来现金流量进行折现确定负债成分的初始金额，再按发行收入扣除负债成分的差额确认权益成分的初始金额。发行费用，应当在负债成分和权益成分之间按其初始确认金额的相对比例进行分摊。

对于投资方，同样要求对取得的可转债的负债部分和权益部分分别进行确认。对负债部分，应按债券的面值，借记可供出售金融资产(成本)，按实际支付的金额，贷记"银行存款"等科目，按差额，借记或贷记"可供出售金融资产(利息调整)"。

(2) 国外的处理方法

根据ED59(国际会计准则59号草案)的规定，对发行可转换债券的处理方法跟我国方法存在很大不同。在发行时也是采用折现的方法，确定权益部分价值，但是发行后处理则是运用实际利率法将"应付债券"调整为债券面值，如债券到期没有实现转换，则要确认留存收益；如实现转换，则将权益部分价值连同债券账面价值一并进行转股处理。

Exercises

1. Which of the following is not a current liability? (   )

A. Account payable.　　　　　　　C. Current-portion of long-term debt.

B. Wages payable.　　　　　　　　D. Bonds payable.

2. A contingent liability should be recorded in the accounts (   ).

A. if the amount can be vaguely estimated.

B. if the amount is due in cash within one year.

C. if the related future event will probably occur.

D. none of above.

3. The discount on a bond payable is (   ).

A. a reduction in interest expense.　　C. a contra account to Bonds payable.

B. an expense at the bond's maturity.　D. an expense account.

4. Issuing bonds is a/an (   ).

A. operating activity.　　　　　　　C. investing activity.

B. financing activity.　　　　　　　D. payment activity.

5. Suppose a company took out a loan from a local bank for $1,000,000. This loan would be paid during the next 5 years. The correct journal entry for this transaction is ( ).

    A. debit account receivable.   C. credit note payable.

    B. debit note receivable.   D. credit cash.

6. Which of the following bonds has the highest interest rate? ( )

    A. Callable bond.   C. Convertible bond.

    B. Mortgage bond.   D. Normal debentures.

7. When the coupon rate is over the market rate, which of following is not correct? ( )

    A. The bond should be issued at a premium.

    B. The bond should be issued at a discount.

    C. The issuer can receive more cash than the bonds' face value.

    D. None of above.

8. Which of the following is not a liability? ( )

    A. Unearned revenue.   C. Pre-paid rent.

    B. Deferred income taxes.   D. Long-term note payable.

9. Which of the following illustrations is correct? ( )

    A. The mortgage bonds are secured by the agreed specific property.

    B. A convertible bond is a type of bond that the holder can convert it into a specified number of shares of common stock in the issuing company or cash of equal value.

    C. A callable bond, gives the bond issuer the right to purchase the bond back from the bondholders before the maturity date of the bond through an embedded call option.

    D. All the above.

10. When the bonds issuer received less cash than the bond's face value, it means that ( ).

    A. the bond is issued at a premium.

    B. the coupon rate is higher than the market rate.

    C. the bond has to be issued at a discount.

    D. the market interest rate is not stable.

11. Name and briefly describe several items that are often classified as current liabilities.

12. "The face amount of a bond is what you can sell it for." Do you agree? Explain.

13. On February 25, Caleny Company had paid the employees compensation for a total $10,000 and still owed them $2,000 until March 25.

(1) Prepare the journal entry for recording the compensation expense for February.

(2) Suppose the total compensation expenses for March is $15,000 and this would be paid on March 25 in total. How much cash would Caleny Company pay on March 25. Prepare the journal entry.

14. Steven Ltd. is a shoe company. It has realized a total $5,000,000 pre-tax earnings for the whole year of 2018. The company had paid income taxes (estimated) of 2018 of $1,800,000 monthly. If the income taxes rate is 40%, calculate how much income tax the company has not yet paid, and prepare the journal entries.

15. The Union, Inc., one of the largest airline companies in the world, had unearned revenues of $450 million on May 30, 2018. Suppose that during June, the Union Inc. has a realized sales revenue of 3 parts: $300 million for pre-paid customers; $200 million for

customers taking the airline in June and $320 million for customers that will take planes in the next month or later.

(1) Prepare journal entries for the unearned revenue during June.

(2) Prepare the journal entry for the realized sales at June.

16. Pepper Co., which is a chain restaurant, had the following items on its December 31, 2018 balance sheet (in thousands):

The Balance Sheet

Pepper Co. Dec. 31, 2018	$In thousands
Cash and cash equivalents	$ 32,000
Account payable	14,500
Deferred income taxes	10,000
Retained earnings	108,900
Accrued expenses	20,100
Prepaid expenses	3,580
Short-term debt	11,580
Current maturities of long-term debt	3,830
Arbitration award	9,880
Long-term debt	50,300
Other long-term liabilities	5,216

Prepare the liabilities section of Pepper Corporation's balance sheet. Include only the items that are properly included in liabilities. Separate current and long-term liabilities.

Chapter 8

Stockholders' Equity

Spotlight

How do you manage your busy life? You may use any of millions of applications (Apps) on a device. HOT company is one of the most famous software companies in the world due to its products (many popular Apps especially mobile games apps), which were sold to many countries, in Asia, Africa, America and Europe. The company started in 2000 and first offered the company's stocks to the public in 2011. Now HOT company operates 20 studios across the world to design and sell its software products. During 2018, the HOT company reported sales of $10 million, net income of $5 million. Because the company had realized net earnings for 10 consecutive years, at the end of 2018, the company issued dividends of $1 million to their stockholders. Table **8-1** showed the balance sheet of HOT company. In this chapter we will show you how to account for HOT's issuance of stock to investors. We will also cover the other elements of stockholders' equity—additional paid-in capital, retained earnings, treasury stock, and dividends.

Table 8-1 The consolidated balance sheet of HOT corporation

HOT Corp. Consolidated Balance Sheet December 31, 2018 (In thousands, except number of shares)	
Assets	
Current assets:	
Total current assets	$ 25,300
Long-term receivables	10,000
Property and equipment, net	32,000
Other assets	22,500
Total assets	$ 89,800
Liabilities and Stockholders' Equity	
Current liabilities	
Total current liabilities	$ 30,500
Long-term debt	10,500
Other long-term liabilities	4,800
Total liabilities	$ 45,800
Stockholders' Equity	

	(Continued)
HOT Corp. **Consolidated Balance Sheet** **December 31, 2018** **(In thousands, except number of shares)**	
Preferred stock, $2 par value, 10,000,000 shares authorized; shares issued and outstanding: none	—
Common stock, $1 par value, 6,000,000 shares authorized; 5,000,000 shares issued and 4,000,000 shares outstanding	4,000
Additional paid-in capital	11,000
Retained earnings	30,000
Treasury stock, at cost (1,000,000 shares)	(1,000)
Total stockholders' equity	44,000
Total liabilities and stockholders' equity	$ 768,870

Text

8.1 Background on Stockholders' Equity

A corporation is a business entity formed under state law with perpetual life. The corporate is a distinct entity with its owners – the **stockholders** or **shareholders**. The stockholders generally have many rights, for example:

(1) Vote. The shareholders have voting rights to influence the decisions made.

(2) Dividends. The shareholders are able to receive dividends that the company distributes to the owners from the net income.

(3) Liquidation. Once a corporation is in liquidation, the shareholders could share the remaining assets after other creditors.

(4) Preemption. It means that the shareholders could acquire more shares of subsequent issues of stock. This right could maintain the shareholders' proportionate ownership in the corporation.

Stockholders' equity represents the stockholders' ownership interest in the assets of a corporation. Stockholders' equity is divided into two main parts:

1. Paid-in capital

This is one part of stockholders' equity, which is the amount the stockholders have contributed to the corporation. Paid-in capital includes the stock accounts and any additional paid-in capital.

2. Retained earnings

This is a big part of stockholders' equity, which is the amount the corporation has earned through profitable operations and has not used for dividends.

The owners' equity of a corporation is divided into shares of **stock**. Because stock represents the corporation's capital, it is often called **capital stock**. As shown in **Table 8-1**, the company had issued 5,000,000 shares with $1 par value to the market. A corporation issues stock certificates to its owners when the company receives their investment. The shareholders could apply dividends by their stock certificates. The basic unit of capital stock is 1 share. A corporation may issue a stock certificate for any number of shares — 56,789 or any other number, but the total number of authorized shares is limited by charter.

To understand the shares of issued stock, you have to understand the relationships among different forms of shares: the authorized shares, issued shares, outstanding shares and treasury stock.

Authorized stock is the maximum number of shares the company can issue under its present charter. Through Table 8-1 we can see HOT is authorized to issue 10,000,000 shares stock.

Issued stock is the number of shares the company has issued to its stockholders. This is a cumulative total from the company's beginning up to the current date. As of December 31, 2018, HOT had issued 5,000,000 shares of its common stock.

Treasury stock. A company's own stock that it has issued and later reacquired is called treasury stock.

Outstanding stock is the number of shares that the stockholders own (that is, the number of shares outstanding in the hands of the stockholders). Outstanding stock is issued stock minus treasury stock. On December 31, 2018, HOT had 4,000,000 shares of common stock outstanding, computed as bellow:

Issued shares	5,000,000
Less: Treasury shares	(1,000,000)
Outstanding shares	4,000,000

The number of **authorized shares** is specified by the government and the state law, which means the corporation could not issue shares without a limited number. When the company issues shares to the investors and receives cash, the shares become **issued shares**. However sometimes the company buys back shares of stock from its own shareholders to use such shares as part of employee bonuses or stock purchase plans. Such shares held by corporations are called **treasury stock**. We shall discuss the details of treasury stock later in this chapter. When we take the number of issued shares and minus the shares of treasury stock, we get the remaining shares that are still in the shareholders hands, except for the corporation itself, called **outstanding shares**.

8.2 Classes of Stock

8.2.1 Common Stock

Common stock is the basic form of capital stock, and the word "stock" is usually understood to mean "common stock". Common stockholders have 4 basic rights of stock ownership as previously discussed. The common stockholders are the owners of the corporation. They invest in the corporation and benefit from the remaining assets at liquidation, so they bear the biggest risk of operation.

8.2.2 Preferred Stock

Preferred stock gives its owners certain advantages and rights over common stockholders, which are mainly illustrated by the fact that preferred stockholders receive dividends before the common stockholders. Moreover, preferred stockholders also receive assets before the common stockholders in the event of liquidation, and they stand to realize payback up to the **liquidation value**. Usually preferred shareholders have a right to receive a fixed cash dividend each year. Owners of preferred stock also have basic stockholder rights, except voting rights. Companies may issue different classes of preferred stock. Each class of stock is recorded on a separate account.

Preferred stock is a hybrid between common stock and long-term debt. Like debt, preferred stock pays a fixed dividend, which is similar to the bond interest. But like stock, the dividend does not have to be paid unless the board of directors declares the dividend. Following Table 8-2 shows the similarities and differences between preferred stock and long-term debt.

Table 8-2 The similarities and differences between preferred stock and long-term debt

	Long-term debt	**Preferred stock**
Similarities	Both pay a specific return to the investor.	
Differences	Interest	Dividend
	Taxable to recipient Tax deductible to the issuing company	Not tax deductible to the issuer. Fully taxed, partly taxed or untaxed to the recipient
	Reduce income before tax	Reduce net income and retained earnings directly
	Have specific maturity dates	Have unlimited life

8.3 Issuing Stock

Most corporations need huge quantities of money to operate or to expand the corporation size. One important financing form is issuing stock to the public. Corporations may sell stock directly to the stockholders or through an underwriter, such as the bank.

8.3.1 Common Stock at Par

In Table 8-1, HOT's common stock carried a par value of $1 per share. If the company issued 500,000 shares at par to the market, the journal entry would be:

Dr: Cash   500,000
   Cr: Common stock   500,000

The effect of this transaction would increase the HOT's assets and stockholders' equity by the same amount as follows:

Assets	=	Liabilities	+	Stockholders' Equity
+500,000	=	0	+	500,000

8.3.2 Common Stock Above Par

The vast majority of corporations set par value low and issue common stock for a price above par. They often separate their common stock recognition into two categories – common stock (par value) and **additional paid-in capital**.

   Suppose HOT's common stock has a par value of $1 per share and the company issued the stock with a market price of $6 per share. The $5 difference between issue price ($6) and par value ($1) is additional paid-in capital. With 500,000 shares issued by par value of $1, HOT's actual entry with a market price of $6 per share to record the issuance of common stock is as follows:

Dr: Cash   3,000,000
   Cr: Common stock   500,000
      Additional paid-in capital   2,500,000

The effect of this transaction would increase the HOT's assets and stockholders' equity by the same amount as follows:

Assets	=	Liabilities	+	Stockholders' Equity
+3,000,000	=	0	+	500,000 + 2,500,000

8.4 Cash Dividends

Dividends are proportional distributions of net income to shareholders in a company, and most of them are cash dividends. Many companies choose to distribute dividends to attract and benefit their shareholders, however, a company must meet both requirements to do so: have enough retained earnings to declare the dividend, and have enough cash to pay cash dividend.

A company's board of directors' votes to approve each dividend and they would not automatically pay dividends regularly. Only once the board of directors has declared a dividend, could the corporation declare a dividend to their shareholders. Once declared, the dividend becomes a legal liability of the company, which becomes a **dividend payable** account.

There are three relevant dates for dividends distributed.

1. Declaration date

On declaration date, the board of directors formally announces that it will pay a dividend, meanwhile, the dividend becomes a liability of the corporation. On this date, the corporation makes a journal entry to record this liability by debiting Retained earnings and crediting Dividends payable. Suppose there are $100,000 cash dividend are declared:

  Dr: Retained earnings   100,000
    Cr: Dividends payable   100,000

2. Date of record

The corporation specifies a date following the declaration date by a few weeks to record shareholders who own stock. All stockholders on that date will receive the dividend. There is no journal entry for the date of record.

3. Payment date

The payment date usually follows the record date by a few days or weeks. On this date the company mails checks to shareholders. However, if a person who hold the stocks on the declaration date, sold them before the date of record, he or she would not receive the dividends. The payment is recorded by debiting **dividends payable** and crediting **Cash**.

  Dr: Dividends payable   100,000
    Cr: Cash   100,000

8.5 Stock dividends

A stock dividend is a proportional distribution by a company of its won stock to its shareholders. The corporation distributes stock dividends to stockholders in proportion to the number of shares they already own.

For example, if you own 100 shares of HOT's stock and the corporation distributes a 10% stock dividend, which means the issuance of one new share for every 10 shares currently owned, you would get 10 (100 *10%) additional shares. As a result, you would own 110 shares of the HOT's common stock. All other HOT's shareholders would also receive 10% additional shares, leaving all common stockholders' proportionate ownership unchanged.

The reasons that corporations choose stock dividends instead of cash dividends might be:

(1) Conserving cash. Companies may wish to continue the dividends to stockholders whilst at the same time retain as much cash as possible to keep operating or expanding the corporation. Therefore, the company may distribute a stock dividend. In addition, the stock dividend would not require stockholders to pay income taxes on such benefits.

(2) Reducing market price per share of common stock distribution of a stock dividend could increase the number of outstanding shares. With a fixed profit, the increasing share numbers could lead the common stock's market price to fall. The lower market price per share could attract more investors.

8.5.1　Large-percentage Stock Dividends

Generally accepted accounting principles (GAAP) require companies to account for stock dividends above 25% of outstanding common shares as **large-percentage stock dividends** and permits these large stock dividends to be recorded at par or stated value. That means that an accounting entry simply transfers the par or stated value of the new shares from the retained earnings account to the common stock account.

Suppose HOT corporation declared and distributed a 30% stock dividend at par value $1 to their shareholders with a total of 400,000 outstanding shares. This transaction would debit retained earnings and credit common stock for the par value of the shares distributed in the dividend.

　　Dr: Retained earnings　　　　　　120,000
　　　Cr: Common stock　　　　　　　120,000

8.5.2　Small-Percentage Stock Dividends

GAAP identifies stock dividends of 25% or less of outstanding common shares as small-percentage stock dividends and suggests accountants account for the dividend at **market value** of the shares distributed, not at par value. That means that an accounting entry transfers the market value of the new shares from the retained earnings account to the common stock account and additional paid-in capital account.

Suppose HOT corporation declared and distributed a 20% stock dividend at par value $1 and market price of $5 to their shareholders with a total of 400,000 outstanding shares. This transaction would debit retained earnings and credit common stock for the par value of the shares distributed in the dividend.

Dr: Retained earnings 400,000
Cr: Common stock 80,000
Additional paid-in capital 320,000

8.5.3 Fractional Shares

Corporations ordinarily issue shares in whole units. But sometimes shareholders are entitled to stock dividends in amounts equal to fractional units. For instance, HOT corporation distributes a 3% stock dividend with a market price of $5 and par value of $1 to their shareholders.

One shareholder has 160 shares, and then the shareholder would be entitled to $160 \times 0.03 = 4.8$ shares. In such a situation, corporations issue additional shares for whole units plus cash equal to the market value of the fractional amount.

As a result, the company would issue 4 shares plus $0.8 \times \$5 = \$4$ cash. The journal entry is as below:

Dr: Retained earnings (4.8×$5) 24
Cr: Common stock, at par (4×$1) 4
Additional paid-in capital(4×$4) 16
Cash 4

Core Words

Stockholders' equity	所有者权益
Paid-in capital	实收资本
Retained earnings	留存收益
Capital stock	股本
Common stock	普通股

Preferred stock	优先股
Par value	面值
Authorized stock	额定股本
Issued stock	已发行股票
Outstanding stock	流通股
Treasury stock	库存股
Cash dividends	现金股利
Stock options	优先认股权
Stock dividends	股票股利
Large-percentage stock dividends	大比例股票股利
Small-percentage stock dividends	小比例股票股利
Fractional shares	零星股

Extended Reading

1. 所有者权益

所有者权益是指资产扣除负债后由所有者应享的剩余权益，即一个会计主体在一定时期所拥有或可控制的具有未来经济利益资源的净额。会计方程式"资产 – 负债 = 所有者权益"清楚地说明了所有者权益实质上是一种剩余权益，是企业全部资产减去全部负债后的差额，体现了企业的产权关系。所有者权益具有以下特征：①所有者权益是企业可长久使用的资金来源，除非发生减资、清算，企业不需要偿还所有者权益。②企业在清算时，所有者权益的清偿列在负债之后。③所有者权益的满足由企业实现的收益程度决定，所有者凭借所有者权益参与利润的分配。 所有者权益的形成渠道有三条：①所有者投入的资本；②所有者投资后的经营增值，如留存收益；③直接计入所有者权益的利得和损失。

2. 留存收益

留存收益是公司在经营过程中所创造的，由于公司经营发展的需要或法定的原因等，没有分配给所有者而留存在公司的盈利。留存收益是指企业从历年实现的利润中提取或留存于企业的内部积累，它来源于企业的生产经营活动所实现的净利润，包括企业的盈余公积金和未分配利润两个部分，其中盈余公积金是有特定用途的累积盈余，未分配利润是没有指定用途的累积盈余。保留盈余的用途有三种：扩充营运规模、投资新的企业、回购股票。

3. 普通股与优先股对比

普通股指的是在公司的经营管理和盈利及财产的分配上享有普通权利的股份，代表满足所有债权偿付要求及优先股东的收益权与求偿权要求后对企业盈利和剩余财产的索取权。它构成了公司资本的基础，是股票的一种基本形式，也是发行量最大、最为重要的一种股票。

优先股是相对于普通股而言的，主要指在利润分红及剩余财产分配的权利方面优先于普通股。优先股股东没有选举及被选举权，一般来说对公司的经营没有参与权。优先股股东不能退股，只能通过优先股的赎回条款被公司赎回，但是能稳定分红的股份。

(1) 股利方面的区别

优先股有固定的股息，不随公司业绩好坏而波动，并且可以先于普通股股东领取股息；而普通股的股利收益没有上下限，视公司经营状况好坏、利润大小而定，公司税后利润在按一定的比例提取了公积金并支付优先股股息后，再按股份比例分配给普通股股东。

(2) 权利方面的区别

优先股的权利范围小，优先股股东一般没有选举权和被选举权，对股份公司的重大经营无投票权；普通股股东一般有出席股东大会的权利，有表决权和选举权、被选举权。

(3) 索偿权的区别

如果公司股东大会需要讨论与优先股有关的索偿权，即优先股的索偿权先于普通股，而次于债权人。

4. 现金股利与股票股利

现金股利是上市公司以货币形式支付给股东的股息红利，也是最普通、最常见的股利形式，如每股派息多少元，就是现金股利。股票股利是公司以增发股票的方式所支付的股利，通常也将其称为"红股"。

现金股利的发放致使公司的资产和股东权益减少同等数额，是企业资产的流出，会减少企业的可用资产，是利润的分配、真正的股利。

股票股利是把原来属于股东所有的留有收益转化为股东所有的投入资本，只不过不能再用来分派股利，实质上是留存利润的凝固化、资本化，并不是真实意义上的股利。股票股利并无资产从企业流出，发给股东的仅仅是其在公司的股东权益份额和价值，股东在公司里占有的权益份额和价值，分不分股票股利都一样，没有变化。

如果用作股票股利的股票在证券市场上是热门股，股价坚挺，新发行作股利的股票又不多，则可望股票市价并不因增发少量股票而有所下降，股票市价基本保持稳定，此时股东可将分得的股票股利在证券市场上抛售，换取现金利益。但这容易引起错觉：认为股票股利与现金股利无异，是实在股利。但这毕竟是假象，实际是在通过拥有多一点股票来体现其在企业中的所有者权益份额情况，出售股票股利的股票就是出售股东在企业所拥有的权益。出售股票的所得，当然有可能一部分包括利润，同时也包括一部分投入资本。

Exercises

1. Preferred stock owners have different rights compared to common stockholders. Which one is not the rights for preferred stock owners? (   )

   A. Receive a cash dividend.　　　C. Liquidation preference.

   B. Voting rights.　　　　　　　　D. Participating.

2. On which date might the company not record a journal entry for the outstanding stock? (   )

   A. Declaration date.　　　　　　C. Payment date.

   B. Date of record.　　　　　　　D. None of them.

3. Tizzy company issued 1,560,000 shares stock on January 15, 2018. The total authorized shares are 2,000,000 shares. The treasury stock that was repurchased by the company was 100,000 shares. How many unissued shares are there on the market? (   )

   A. 340,000 shares.　　　　　　　C. 1,460,000 shares.

   B. 1,900,000 shares.　　　　　　D. 440,000 shares.

4. Tizzy company issued 1,560,000 shares stock on January 15, 2018. The total authorized shares are 2,000,000 shares. Tizzy company planned to issue the others (440,000 shares) in the second quarter. The treasury stock repurchased by the company was 100,000 shares. How many outstanding shares are there on the market? (   )

   A. 340,000 shares.　　　　　　　C. 1,460,000 shares.

   B. 1,900,000 shares.　　　　　　D. 440,000 shares.

5. Which of the following is false? (   )

A. Authorized shares are the total number of shares that may legally be issued under the articles of incorporation.

B. Unissued shares are the number of shares sold to the public.

C. Outstanding shares are shares remaining in the hands of shareholders.

D. Treasury stock is a corporation's issued stock that has subsequently been repurchased by the issuing company.

6. At liquidation, which kind of owners have the last liquidation preference? (   )

A. Owners of unsubordinated debentures.

B. Owners of common stock.

C. Owners of subordinated debentures.

D. Owners of accounts payable.

7. Referring to the differences between bond and preferred stock, which one is not true among the following? (   )

A. The bond interest is not tax deductible to the issuing company.

B. The preferred stock has unlimited life.

C. The bond interest reduces income before tax.

D. The cash dividend of preferred stock reduces net income and retained earnings directly.

8. A company paid the large percentage stock dividend to shareholders on December 20. Which of the following accounts should the company credit?(   )

A. Retained earnings.   C. Cash dividend.

B. Common stock.   D. additional paid-in capital.

9. Spencer Ltd. issued small-percentage stock dividends. Which of the following is the right journal entry? (   )

A. Dr: common stock   Cr: retained earnings (par value)

B. Dr: common stock, additional paid-in capital   Cr: retained earnings

C. Dr: retained earnings (par value)   Cr: common stock

D. Dr: retained earnings   Cr: common stock, additional paid-in capital

10. Which of the following is correct concerning stock dividends? (   )

A. Stock dividends are distributions of cash to stockholders.

B. Stock dividends have no effect on total stockholders' equity.

C. Stock dividends reduce the total assets of the company.

D. Stock dividends increase the corporation's total liabilities

11. Conda Food is a chain supermarket in USA. Conda started issuing its first common stock at NYSE on May 5, 2010. Assume Conda issued 1,000,000 shares with par value of $9. The market price of the issued stock is $12. Prepare the journal entry on the issue date.

12. In 2018, Hong company declared dividends of $0.1 per share for a total of 10 million outstanding shares. Assume the company declared dividends on November 15, 2018, recorded stockholder on December 1, and distributed the dividends on December 15. Prepare the journal entries related to the necessary dates.

13. Suppose KAKA corporation declared and distributed a 30% stock dividend at par value $0.1 and market price of $4 to their shareholders with a total of 200,000 outstanding shares. Prepare the journal entries for this stock dividend distribution.

14. A software company named YOYO just distributed a 3% stock dividend with a market price of $5 and par value of $1 to their shareholders. Suppose Mr. Yang had purchased 130 shares of the company's stock before. When the company distributed this stock dividend, how did Mr. Yang's stock change? Please list the calculation process and make a journal entry for this stock dividend distribution.

Chapter 9

Revenues and Expenses

Spotlight

Tom and Anna just graduated from a Finance and Economic College in Seattle, they planned to open a café in the South district of Seattle. They found a shop on the corner of a street that is suitable because the number of pedestrians on this street is tremendous. Due to the prominent geographical position of this shop, the rent fees are relatively expensive. The first big decision for them was whether to choose this shop or not. After discussion, they decided to rent this shop and then planned to raise the price of every cup of coffee to recover the expensive rent fees and they believe that the selling price is acceptable in Seattle. After they had finished the decorations and preparations for the inventories and equipment, their Tika café store opened on January 1, 2018. Except for the above preparations they had already completed, more complex situations would arise in the daily operation. In this chapter, we take their Tika café as an example to learn how they record revenues and expenses.

Table 9-1 shows the income statement of Tika café after one-month of operation.

Table 9-1 income statement of December 31, 2018 on Tika Café

Tika café consolidated Statements of Earnings ($ in thousands) December 31, 2018	
Net Revenues:	
Net operating revenues	$13,300
Other income and gains (net)	280
Total net revenue	13,580
Cost of sales	5,800
Store rent expenses	2,400
Other operating expenses	2,000
Depreciation expenses	550
General and administrative expenses	800
Other expenses	5
Income before income taxes	2,025
Income taxes expenses	810
Net income	$1,215

Revenues and Expenses — Chapter 9

Text

9.1 Accrual Basis and Cash Basis

The timing of revenue recognition is so important because the timing decides the final net income at the end of an accounting period. The revenue recognition affects net income in two ways: ①it directly affects net income because it is one element of the calculation —— net income equals revenues minus expenses. ②It indirectly affects net income for the reason that it determines when a company records certain expenses. According to the matching principle, a company reports the cost of the items sold in the same accounting period in which it recognizes the related revenues.

The revenues or expenses recognition are founded on two main accounting basis: **accrual basis** and **cash basis**.

9.1.1 Accrual Basis

Accrual basis accounting records the impact of a transaction when it occurs, which means that the recognition must meet two conditions: first, the goods or services must be delivered to the customers, that is, the revenue must be earned; second, cash or an asset virtually assured of being converted into cash must be received, that is, the revenue must be realized. In other word, when the business performs a service, makes a sale, or incurs an expense, the accountant records the transaction, even if the business receives or pays no cash.

9.1.2 Cash Basis

Cash basis accounting records only cash transactions, such as cash receipts and cash payments, that is, cash receipts are regarded as revenues, and cash payments are treated as expenses without considering the accounting period.

The majority of accounting principles across the world require accrual basis accounting because it records revenues when the revenues are earned and recognizes the expenses as the expenses are incurred, not depending on the cash inflow or outflow.

9.2 Measurement of Sales Revenue

After deciding the timing to recognize revenues, accountants must determine the amount of revenue to record. **Sales revenue** account is usually recognized in two ways: **cash sales** and **credit sales**.

A cash sale means a company makes a transaction receiving cash immediately as the goods or services are delivered. A cash sale increases a company's sales revenue, which is an account in income statement, and also increases cash, which is a balance sheet account.

A credit sale is recorded on open account, which means that the company realized revenues but did not yet receive cash. The credit sale transaction increases **accounts receivable** account instead of cash account, which is also a balance sheet account.

Suppose the Tika café had earned $1,000 cash on January 10, 2018, the journal entry for that day's revenue recognition would be:

 Dr: Cash   1,000
  Cr: Sales revenue   1,000

However, as well as the cash sales on January 10, 2018, there is also a credit sale for $400, which would be paid at the end of the month, the journal entry for such a transaction would be different from cash sales. The journal entry would be:

 Dr: Accounts receivable   400
  Cr: Sales revenue   400

9.3 Merchandise Returns and Allowances

The sales revenue recognition above seems easy, however, sometimes the amount of revenue recognized at the point of sale is not the same as the cash finally received. Suppose the customer returns the merchandise due to the unsatisfactory color or quality, the company has to return part of or all cash receipt or reduce the recognized revenue.

Suppose customers return two bags of coffee beans to Tika café due to the incorrect flavor for a total of $80. The journal entry for this return would be:

 Dr: Sales returns and allowances   80
  Cr: cash   80

In another situation, instead of returning merchandise, the customer might demand a reduction in the selling price. For instance, a customer was unhappy with the scratches on the coffee machine, and then asked for a discount on the selling price. Tika café accounts for such complaints by granting a sales allowance.

Suppose the customer was offered a price reduction of $20 due to the scratches on the coffee machine. The journal entry for the sellers' sale allowance is:

 Dr: Sales returns and allowances   20

Cr: cash   20

The two transactions above regarding the sale returns and allowances would affect the income statement as follows:

Gross sales	$1,000
Deduct: Sales returns and allowances	100
Net sales	$ 900

The **sales returns and allowance account** is a contra account of the **sales revenue** account. Sellers use a contra account to record changes in the level of returns and allowances. Such level of returns and allowances can be used to track customer's tastes and assess the quality of products and services. Because returns happen after the sales, managers usually separate the returns and allowances account to avoid going back and changing the original entries for the sale, which could lead to a messy and unreliable process.

9.4 Cash and Trade Discounts

In addition to returns and allowances, cash and trade discounts also reduce original sales.

9.4.1 Trade Discounts

Trade discounts usually refer to the price reduction on large-volume purchases. The company might offer a price discount on total merchandise sales over $100,000.

Suppose Tika café organized a sales activity — coffee beans 3 bags for 2, which means if customers bought 2 bags of coffee beans, they can get one bag for free. Because the price reduction is before the transaction, the journal entry for such revenue recognition could be recorded by the price after discount directly, not necessarily recording the original price.

9.4.2 Cash Discounts

In contrast to trade discounts, cash discounts are rewards for prompt payment. Sellers quote the terms of the discount in various ways on the invoice.

Following is typical cash discount symbol.

n/30   The full billed price (net price) is due on the thirtieth day after the invoice date.

1/5,n/30   A 1% discount can be taken for payment within 5 days of the invoice date; otherwise, the full billed price is due in 30 days.

15 E.O.M   The full price is due within 15 days after the end of the month of sale; an invoice dated December 20 is due January 15.

Suppose Tika café had made a credit sale of one hundred bags of coffee beans to a food retailer for $2,600 on February 20, 2018. The agreed payment date was one week later on February 27, 2018. The Tika café also gave the retailer a cash discount of 1/3, n/7. The retailer made a full payment for the coffee beans for February 22, 2018. The journal entry for this transaction would be:

February 20, 2018

    Dr: Accounts receivables   2,600

        Cr: Sales revenue   2,600

February 22, 2018

    Dr: Cash   2,340

        Cash discounts   260

        Cr: Accounts receivables   2,600

9.5 Expenses

We have learned how to recognize revenues on the accrual basis. What about expenses? We can categorise expenses into two types: ①expenses linked with the revenues earned that period; ②expenses linked with the time period itself.

The first one usually refers to cost of sales. We recognize and record cost of sales in the same period that we recognize their related sales revenues.

It is difficult to link some other expenses directly to specific revenues. For example, rent expenses are always paid before using the building, which becomes a pre-paid expense. For example, a one-year renting could benefit the company the whole year, so the rent expense should be allocated to every month. Such expenses support a company's operations for a given period, as do similar expenses including advertisement expense, administrative expense, depreciation expense, and so on. We called these expenses **period costs**. We record period costs as expenses in the period in which the company incurs them.

9.5.1 Expiration of Unexpired Costs

Some pre-paid assets expire due to the passage of time. For example, **pre-paid rent** is an asset account on the balance sheet. As the corporation consumes the asset, such assets should be reduced from the balance and treated as expenses on the income statement. The key characteristic of unexpired cost is that a transaction in the past created an asset, and subsequent consumption serves to adjust the value of the asset. Other examples of adjusting for asset expirations include the write-

Revenues and Expenses Chapter 9

offs to expense of such assets as prepaid insurance and office supplies inventory.

Tika café rented a store on January 1, 2018 for $2,400,000 for the whole year of 2018. The rent fees should be regarded as a pre-paid asset listed in the current assets of the balance sheet because such fees would support the corporation for one year. Then, as time passes, the value of the assets reduce, which means that the pre-paid rent is transferred into expense in the income statement. The journal entry for this rent payment and adjustment is:

January 1, 2018
   Dr: Pre-paid rent   2,400,000
      Cr: Cash   2,400,000

subsequent ending of months
   Dr: Rent expenses   200,000
      Cr: Pre-paid rent   200,000

9.5.2 Accrual of Unrecorded Expenses

Wages are a typical example of accrual expenses. Employees' salary is a liability that grows moment to moment as employees perform their duties. In other words, as the employees provide services, the accrual wages expenses are incurred.

The wages expenses grow hourly and daily, but accountants record these expenses only when they prepare financial statements. As a result, they make adjustments to bring each accrued expense account up-to-date at the end of the period, just before they prepare the formal financial statement. These adjustments are necessary to accurately match the expense to the period in which they help generate revenues.

1. Accounting for Payment of Wages

Employees in Tika could receive their salary at the end of month. Suppose the wages for every month are $60,000. How does Tika record such expenses at the end of month?

   Dr: Wages expense   60,000
      Cr: Cash   60,000

2. Accounting for Accrual of Wages

Assume that Tika café paid employees their salary in the middle of every month at 15th. When accountants prepare the monthly financial statement, there still have half of the salaries not yet to be paid to the employees which become liabilities. Suppose on the June 30, 2018, Tika café still owe its employees $30,000 not yet paid. The journal entry for this liability would be:

```
Dr: Wages expense                    30,000
    Cr: Accrued wages payable            30,000
```

There are many similar accrual expenses as wages expenses, like **accrued interest payable** and accrued **income taxes payable, and so on**. The journal entries for such accrual expenses are similar to wages expenses.

Core Words

Revenues	收入
Expenses	费用
Matching	配比原则
Sales revenue	业务收入
Cost of sales/cost of goods sold	业务成本
Cash discounts	现金折扣
Trade discounts	商业折扣
Credit sales	赊销
Cash sales	现销
Adjustments	期末调整
Depreciation expenses	折旧费用
Administrative expenses	管理费用
Period costs	期间费用
Pre-paid expenses	预付账款
Accrued wages payable	应付职工薪酬
Accrued interest payable	应付利息
Accrued income tax payable	应交所得税费

Extended Reading

1. 配比原则

配比原则，即某个会计期间或某个会计对象所取得的收入应与为取得该收入所发生的费用、成本相匹配，以正确计算在该会计期间该会计主体所获得的净损益。配比原则作为会计要素确认要求，用于利润确定。会计主体的经济活动会带来一定的收入，也必然要发生相应的费用。有所得必有所费，所费是为了所得，两者是对立的统一，利润正是所得比较所费的结果。配比原则的依据是受益原则，即谁受益，费用归谁负担。受益原则承认得失之间存在因果关系，但并非所有费用与收入之间都存在因果关系，必须按照配比原则区分有因果联系的直接成本费用和没有直接联系的间接成本费用。直接费用与收入进行直接配比来确定本期损益；间接费用则通过判断而采用适当合理的标准，先在各个产品和各期收入之间进行分摊，然后用收入配比来确定损益。

2. 现金折扣与商业折扣的区别

现金折扣又称销售折扣。为督促顾客尽早付清货款而提供的一种价格优惠。现金折扣的表示方式为：2/10，1/20，n/30(即10天内付款，货款折扣2%；20天内付款，货款折扣1%，30天内全额付款)。现金折扣发生在销货之后，是一种融资性质的理财费用，因此现金折扣不得从销售额中扣除。商业折扣，是指企业根据市场供需情况或针对不同顾客，在商品标价上给予的扣除。商业折扣是企业最常用的促销方式之一。企业为了扩大销售、占领市场，对于批发商给予商业折扣，采用销量越多、价格越低的促销策略，也就是我们通常所说的"薄利多销"，如购买5件，销售价格折扣10%；购买10件，折扣20%等。其特点是折扣在实现销售的同时发生，商品折扣从销售额中扣除。

3. 期末账项调整

期末账项调整即期末结账前，按照权责发生制原则，确定本期的应得收入和应负担的费用，并据以对账簿记录的有关账项做出必要调整的会计处理方法。账项调整的目的是为了正确地分期计算损益，即正确地划分相邻会计期间的收入和费用，使应属报告期的收入和成本费用相配比，以便正确地结算各期的损益和考核各会计期间的财务成果。

Exercises

1. Which of the following about revenues is correct? (   )

A. Revenues decrease in liabilities resulting from paying off loans.

B. Revenues increase in retained earnings resulting from selling products or performing services.

C. Revenues increase in paid-in capital resulting from the owners investing in the business.

D. All of the above.

2. The timing of revenue recognition is so important because (   ).

A. it directly affects the net income.

B. it indirectly affects the net income.

C. it also affects the recognition of related expense.

D. all of the above.

3. Under GAAP and IFRS, accounting is based on (   ).

A. cash basis.   C. accrual basis.

B. asset basis.   D. account basis.

4. Suppose a company made a credit sale for $400,000 to its customers, which of the following journal entries is correct for this transaction? (   )

A. Debit cash.   C. Credit cost of sales.

B. Debit accounts receivable.   D. Credit notes receivable.

5. Assume a customer was not satisfied with the product's quality because there were some obvious scratches on it. The customer asked for a price reduction of $20. Which of the following journal entries is correct? (   )

A. Debit accounts receivable.   C. Credit sales returns and allowance.

B. Debit cash.   D. Credit cash.

6. In which situation does the accountant not need to make a new journal entry to record the allowances or discounts? (   )

A. Sales returns.   C. Trade discount.

B. Sales allowances.   D. Cash discount.

7. Suppose a company had made a credit sale for $3,000 on February 2, 2018. The company gave the customer a cash discount for 1/5, *n*/10. The customer made a full payment within 3 days. The journal entry for this payment would be: (   )

A. Dr: Cash

　　Cr: cash discount and account receivable

B. Dr: Cash discount

　　Cr: account receivable and sales return

C. Dr: Account receivable

    Cr: Cash and cash discount

D. None of the above.

8. Assuming the conditions of the 7th question, how much cash did the company receive after the customer's payment? (　)

A. 0.

B. $3,000.

C. $30.

D. $2,970.

9. Which of the following regarding the expiration of unexpired costs is false? (　)

A. Pre-paid rent is an asset account.

B. The balance of the pre-paid rent account would be reduced by the passage of time.

C. The pre-paid rent account would be converted into rent expense during the given period.

D. None of the above.

10. Which of the following expenses can be related to a certain period when the revenues are realized? (　)

A. Wages expense.

B. Income taxes expense.

C. Cost of sales.

D. Insurance expense.

11. Distinguish between a cash discount and a trade discount.

12. Revenue recognition, cash discounts, and returns.

A bookstore sold 1,000 practice books to a primary school on February 20. The practice books were delivered on February 25, at which time the bookstore sent a bill to the school requesting payment of $50 per book. The bookstore also allowed a 2% cash discount if the school could make the payment within 10 days. The primary school made the full payment on March 1. However, on March 10, the primary school returned 60 books for a full cash refund.

Prepare the journal entries for the bookstore on (a) February 20, (b) February 25, (c)

March 1, and (d) March 10.

13. Make journal entries for the following transactions:

(1) Sale of inventory, $40,000 on open account and $20,000 for cash. The cost of merchandise is $30,000.

(2) Rent expense was recognized for the month for $10,500.

(3) Insurance expense was recognized for the month for $2,000.

(4) Return part of inventories due to the bad quality, which are worth $5,000.

(5) Asked for a price reduction due to the poor color of the products of $50.

(6) Sold 10,000 pens with the price of $3 per unit, and offered a trade discount of $2.5 per unit when purchasing volume is over 1,000 units.

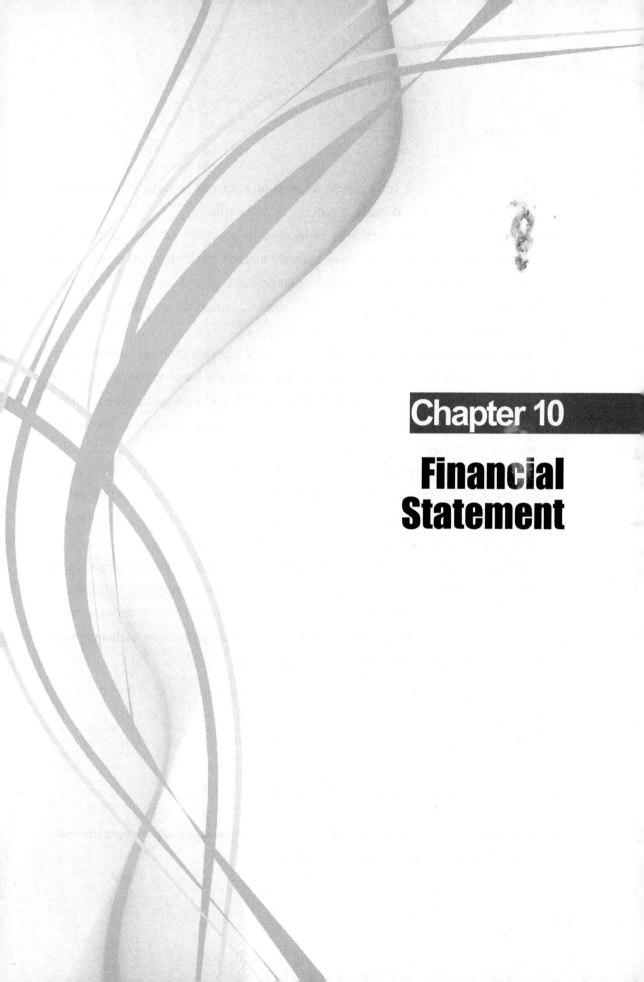

Chapter 10

Financial Statement

Spotlight

A financial statement (or financial report) is a formal record of the financial activities and position of a business, a person, or other entities.

Relevant financial information is presented in a structured manner and in a form that is easy to understand. They typically include basic financial statements, accompanied by a management discussion and analysis.

A balance sheet or statement of financial position, reports on a company's assets, liabilities, and owners' equity at a certain point in time.

An income statement or statement of comprehensive income, statement of revenue & expense, P&L or profit and loss report, reports on a company's income, expenses, and profits over a period of time. A profit and loss statement provides information on the operation of the enterprise. This includes sales and the various expenses incurred during the stated period.

A Statement of changes in equity or equity statement or statement of retained earnings, reports on the changes in equity of the company during the stated period.

A cash flow statement reports on a company's cash flow activities, particularly its operating, investing and financing activities.

For large corporations, these statements may be complex and may include an extensive set of footnotes to the financial statements and management discussion and analysis. The notes typically describe each item on the balance sheet, income statement and cash flow statement in further detail. Notes to financial statements are considered an integral part of the financial statements.

Text

10.1 Overview of a Financial Statement

Stakeholders need to obtain information about the bussiness to make the right decisions. The financial statement is the tool to get information.

Chapter 10 Financial Statement

There are four main kinds of financial statements:
- Income statement
- Statement of retained earnings
- Balance sheet
- Statement of cash flow

What would stakeholders want to know about a company? How can we obtain information from these financial statements? The role of each financial statement is shown in Table 10-1.

Table 10-1 Information from the financial statements

Question	Financial Statement	Answer
What's the performance of a company during the year?	Income statement	Revenues−Expenses
Why did the retained earnings change?	Statement of retained earnings	Beginning retained earnings +Net income (−Net loss) −Dividends
What's the financial position at year end?	Balance sheet	Assets=Liabilities+ Stockholder's equity
What's the status of cash flow during the year?	Statement of cash flow	Operating cash flow ± Investing cash flows ± Financing cash flow = Increase (decrease) in cash

10.2 Formats for Financial Statements

10.2.1 Income Statement Formats

1. Single-step income statement

In single-step format, all the revenues are listed together under a heading, such as Revenues. All the expenses are listed together under a heading, such as Expenses. There is only one step to calculate the net income (or net loss). A single-step income statement is shown in Table 10-2.

Table 10-2 Single-step income statement

Income Statement	
March 31, 2019	
(Amounts in thousands)	
Revenues:	
Net operation revenues	7,785
Other income	89
Total net revenues	7,876
Expenses:	
Cost of goods sold	3,179

(Continued)

Income Statement	
Store operating expenses	2,688
Other operating expenses	260
Depreciation ex penses	387
Administrative expenses	473
Total operating expenses	6,987
Income before income taxes	889
Income tax expense	325
Net income	562

2. Multi-step income statement

In multi-step income statement, there is no heading like revenues or expenses. Instead, gross profit, income from operations, income before tax, and net income are highlighted for emphasis. A multi-step income statement is shown in Table 10-3.

Table 10-3 Multi-step income statement

Income Statement	
March 31, 2019	
(Amounts in thousands)	
Net operation revenues	7,785
Cost of goods sold	3,179
Gross profit	4,680
Store operating expenses	2,688
Other operating expenses	260
Depreciation expenses	387
Administrative expenses	473
Total operating expense	3,808
Income from operations	800
Other income	89
Income before income taxes	889
Income tax expense	325
Net income	562

10.2.2 Balance Sheet Formats

1. Report format balance sheet

The report format lists the assets at the top, followed by the liabilities and stockholder's equity below. A report format balance sheet is shown in Table 10-4.

Financial Statement

Table 10-4 Report format balance sheet

Balance Sheet

December 31, 2019

(Amounts in thousands)

Assets

Current assets:

Cash and cash equivalents	311
Short-term investments	145
Accounts receivable	245
Inventories	622
Other current assets	211
Total current assets	1,534
Long-term investments	225
Property, plant, and equipment, net	2,288
Intangible assets	199
Other assets	165
Total assets	4,411

Liabilities and Stockholders' Equity

Current liabilities:

Account payable	450
Short-term notes payable	980
Total current liabilities	1,430
Long-term debt	2
Other long-term liabilities	68
Total liabilities	1,500

Stockholders' equity:

Common stock	500
Retained earnings	2,000
Other equity	411
Total stockholders' equity	2,911
Total liabilities and shareholders' equity	4,411

2. Account format balance sheet

The account format lists the assets on the left, and the liabilities and stockholder's equity on the right in the same way that a T-account appears.

An account format balance sheet is shown in Table 10-5.

Table 10-5 Account format balance sheet

Balance Sheet

December 31, 2019

(Amounts in thousands)

Assets		Liabilities	
Current assets:		Current liabilities:	
Cash and cash equivalents	311	Account payable	450
Short-term investments	145	Short-term notes payable	980
Accounts receivable	245	Total current liabilities	1,430
Inventories	622	Long-term debt	2
Other current assets	211	Other long-term liabilities	68
Total current assets	1,534	Total liabilities	1,500
Long-term investments	225	**Stockholders' Equity:**	
Property, plant, and equipment, net	2,288	Common stock	500
Intangible assets	199	Retained earnings	2,000
Other assets	<u>165</u>	Other equity	<u>411</u>
Total assets	<u>4,411</u>	Total stockholders' equity	<u>2,911</u>
		Total liabilities and shareholders' equity	<u>4,411</u>

Financial statements are related and compiled in order. The relationship is shown in Table 10-6.

Table 10-6 The relationship of the financial statements

Income Statement
December 31, 2018

(Amounts in thousands)

Revenue:		
Service revenue		330
Expenses:		
Salary expense	177	
Depreciation expense-equipment	20	
Depreciation expense-building	10	
Supplies expense	4	
Miscellaneous expense	<u>13</u>	<u>224</u>
Income before income tax		106
Income tax expense		<u>35</u>
Net income		<u>71</u>

Statement of retained earnings
December 31, 2018

(Amounts in thousands)

Retained earnings, December 31, 2017	193
Add: Net income	<u>71</u>
	264
Less: Dividends	<u>(65)</u>
Retained earnings, December 31, 2018	<u>199</u>

Balance Sheet
December 31, 2018

(Amounts in thousands)

Assets			Liabilities	
Cash		198	Accounts payable	380
Accounts receivable		382	Salary payable	5
Supplies		2	Unearned service revenue	13
Equipment	100		Income tax payable	<u>35</u>
Less: Accumulated depreciation	<u>(60)</u>	40	Total liabilities	433
Building	250		**Stockholders' Equity**	
Less: Accumulated depreciation	<u>(140)</u>	110	Common stock	100
Total assets		<u>732</u>	Retained earnings	<u>199</u>
			Total stockholders' equity	299
			Total liabilities and stockholders' equity	<u>732</u>

The order to prepare financial statements:

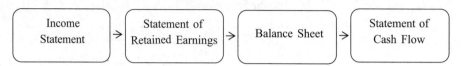

Core Words

Income statement	利润表
Statement of retained earnings	留存收益表
Balance sheet	资产负债表
Statement of cash flow	现金流量表
Single-step income statement	单步式利润表
Multi-step income statement	多步式利润表
Report format balance sheet	报告式资产负债表
Account format balance sheet	账户式资产负债表

Extended Reading

1. 财务报表

财务报表是以会计准则为规范编制的，向所有者、债权人、政府、其他有关各方及社会公众等外部信息使用者反映会计主体财务状况和经营成果的报告性文件。

财务报表包括资产负债表、利润表、现金流量表、所有者权益变动表和附注。财务报表是财务报告的主要部分。

资产负债表反映企业资产、负债及资本的期末状况，同时还反映企业的长期偿债能力、短期偿债能力和利润分配能力等。

利润表又称损益表，用来反映企业本期收入、费用和应该计入当期利润的利得及损失的金额和结构情况。

现金流量表反映企业现金流量的来龙去脉，分为经营活动、投资活动及筹资活动三部分。

所有者权益变动表反映本期企业所有者权益总量的增减变动情况及结构变动的情况，特别是要反映直接计入所有者权益的利得和损失。

财务报表附注一般包括如下项目：企业的基本情况、财务报表编制基础、遵循企业会计准则的声明、重要的会计政策和会计估计、会计政策和会计估计变更及差错的更正说明和重要的报表项目说明。

2. 关于财务报表的中外差异

在我国，企业的利润表采用多步式进行编制，资产负债表采用账户式进行编制，而国际会计准则中没有明确的要求。以美国为例，企业可以自主选择单步式或多步式对利润表进行列报，也可以根据企业自身需要将单步式和多步式进行混合。同样，企业也可以自主选择报告式或账户式对资产负债表进行编制。

另外，对于所有者权益的披露，我国编制的是所有者权益变动表，而美国则编制留存收益表。

Exercises

1. Which of the following is included in gross profit? (　　)

A. Cost of goods sold.　　　　　C. Depreciation expense.

B. Operating expense.　　　　　D. Administrative expense.

2. Which of the following will not affect operating expense? (　　)

A. Depreciation expense.　　　　C. Cost of goods sold.

B. Administrative expense.　　　D. Rent expense.

3. Which of the following is the most liquid current asset? (　　)

A. Cash and cash equivalent.　　C. Accounts receivable.

B. Short-term investment.　　　D. Inventory.

4. Which of the following is a long-term asset? (　　)

A. Inventory.　　　　　　　　　C. Investment.

B. Account receivable.　　　　　D. Intangibles.

5. What is included in the statements of cash flow? (　　)

A. Operating cash flow.　　　　　C. Financing cash flow.

B. Investing cash flow.　　　　　D. All of the above.

6. What is the right order of accounting work? ( )

A. Ledger, journal, trail balance, financial statement.

B. Journal, ledger, trail balance, financial statement.

C. Financial statement, ledger, journal, trail balance.

D. Journal, trail balance, ledger, financial statement.

7. What is the right order to prepare financial statement? ( )

A. Income statement, statement of retained earnings, balance sheet, statement of cash flow.

B. Income statement, balance sheet, statement of retained earnings, statement of cash flow.

C. Balance sheet, income statement, statement of retained earnings, statement of cash flow.

D. Statement of cash flow, income statement, statement of retained earnings, balance sheet.

8. Which of the following is reported in paid in capital account? ( )

A. Dividend.
B. Administrative expense.
C. Preferred stock.
D. Cash and cash equivalent.

9. Which of the following appears on both a single-step and a multi-step income statement? ( )

A. Sales.
B. Operating income.
C. Gross profit.
D. Cost of goods sold.

10. Which of the following is the investing activity of statement of cash flow? ( )

A. Payment of cash to suppliers for inventory.

B. Payment of cash to purchase outstanding capital stock.

C. Receipt of cash from the issuance of bonds payable.

D. Receipt of cash from the sale of equipment.

11. Identify the 2 basic categories of items on an income statement.

12. What do we call the bottom line of the income statement?

Chapter 11

Auditing

Spotlight

The word "audit" is derived from a Latin word "audire" which means "to hear". During Medieval Times when manual book-keeping was prevalent, auditors in Britain used to hear the accounts read out aloud for them and checked that the organization's accounting record were not negligent or fraudulent. Moyer identified that the most important duty of the auditor was to detect fraud. Chatfield documented that early United States auditing was viewed mainly as verification of bookkeeping detail.

An external auditor performs an audit, in accordance with specific laws or rules, of the financial statements of a company, a government entity, other legal entities, or organizations, and is independent of the entity being audited. Users of these entities' financial information, such as investors, government agencies, and the general public, rely on the external auditor to present an unbiased and independent audit report.

The manner of appointment, the qualifications, and the format of reporting by an external auditor are defined by statute, which varies according to jurisdiction. External auditors must be members of one of the recognized professional accountancy bodies. External auditors normally address their reports to the shareholders of a corporation. In the United States, certified public accountants are the only authorized non-governmental external auditors who may perform audits and attestations on an entity's financial statements and provide reports on such audits for public review.

For public companies listed on stock exchanges in the United States, the *Sarbanes-Oxley Act* (SOX) has imposed stringent requirements on external auditors in their evaluation of internal controls and financial reporting. In many countries external auditors of nationalized commercial entities are appointed by an independent government body such as the Comptroller and Auditor General. Securities and Exchange Commissions may also impose specific requirements and roles on external auditors, including strict rules to establish independence.

11.1 Audit Framework

11.1.1 Necessity of Auditing

With the development of market economy, the ownership and management of enterprises have gradually separated. The owner no longer participates in daily management of the enterprise. So how do shareholders understand the day-to-day operations of the business? They can get information from the financial statements. However, there is a conflict in this process. Directors are in charge of the management of an entity as well as preparing the financial statement of this entity. External audits can not ensure that financial statements are objective, free from bias and manipulation and relevant to the needs of the users by reviewing the financial statements. But auditing can increase people's confidence in using statements. External audits can help to protect shareholders' interest.

11.1.2 The Nature of Audit

According to ISA 200, showld be purpose of audit is to enhance the degree of confidence of intended users in the financial statements. This is achieved by the expression of an opinion by the auditor on whether the financial statements are prepared, in all material respects, in accordance with an applicable financial reporting framework.

Auditors do not certify the financial statements or guarantee that the financial statements are correct. They only give a reasonable assurance that the information audited is free of material misstatement.

11.1.3 Advantages of Audit

External auditors should be completely independent from the business. They are hired to determine whatever the company's financial statements comply with generally accepted accounting principles. Auditors examine the clients' financial statements and the underlying transactions in order to form a professional opinion of the financial statements. The advantages of audit can be summarized as follows:

(1) Disputes between management are easier to resolve. This is because that an audit helps to provide an independent examination of financial statements. Therefore the report on

the results of the operation is more reliable.

(2) Major changes in ownership may be facilitated if past accounts contain an unqualified auditing report.

(3) Auditing can help an entity to identify problems and to give constructive advice to management on improving the efficiency of the business.

(4) Auditing can help third parties obtain fair information. For example, the tax department and bank.

11.1.4 Disadvantages of Audit

The disadvantages of audit can be summarized as follows:

① The audit fees. It is worth noting that auditing does not help companies improve profit. On the contrary, auditing produces fees.

② The auditing procedure will affect the normal working schedule of the enterprise. The audit involves the client's staff and management in giving their time in providing information to the auditor. A professional auditor should therefore plan his audit procedure carefully to minimize the disruption.

11.1.5 Stages of Audit

1. Planning

There are two main substances in the planning process. One is to compile the annual audit project plan. Another is to compile the audit work plan, which mainly includes the audit target, scope, content, and emphasis.

2. Audit implementation stage

(1) Interim audit

This is carried out during the period of review. Work tends to focus on **risk assessment** and on documenting and testing internal control. Some substantive procedures can also be carried out but these are limited.

(2) Final audit

It takes place after the year end. It focuses on the audit of the financial statements and concludes with the auditor issuing a report.

3. Reporting

It is the final stage in which the auditor expresses an opinion in the financial statements.

11.2 Professional Ethics and Codes of Conduct

Ethics concern what is morally wrong or right. It is not a legal requirement but it is advisable to follow. Why?

● It enhances the users confidence that the auditor is functioning according to a code of ethics.

● The auditor needs the codes of ethics to make sure that he is worthy of a level of trust.

● It is necessary to uphold the level and quality of work performed.

● The rules deter misconduct and departures from ethical codes and professional conduct.

● If codes of ethics are not applied, disciplinary actions may be taken.

● The maintenance of professional codes of ethics helps the accountancy profession to act in the public interest by providing appropriate regulation of members.

11.2.1 The Fundamental Principles

1. Integrity

Members should be straightforward and honest in all professional/business relationships. It is not allowed to provide false, misleading or incomplete information.

2. Objectivity

Members do not allow bias or conflict of interest in business judgements. Conflict of interest and influences should be avoided.

3. Professional competence and due care

A professional accountant shall maintain professional knowledge and skills at the level required to ensure that a client or a employer receives competent professional service based on current developments in practice, legislation, techniques and act diligently in accordance with applicable technical and professional standards.

4. Confidentiality

Information on clients should not be disclosed without appropriate specific authority.

5. Professional behavior

Members should comply with relevant laws and avoid actions discrediting the profession.

11.2.2 Independence

Independence is the cornerstone of the auditing profession.

Why is it necessary for external auditors to be independent?

Basis of independence:

(1) Agency theory: because they act on behalf of the owners (shareholders) and report on the financial statement prepared by appointed management staff for the benefit of the shareholders.

(2) Statute: national legislation requires it.

(3) The ACCA rules of professional conduct: require that auditors are independent and they are seen to be independent. The rules cover a number of areas in which auditors' independence may be or be seen to be impaired.

(4) Impair objectivity: if they are not independent, their objectivity and ability to form an opinion on the financial statement is impaired.

(5) Instill confidence: auditors must be seen to be independent because if they are not independent, the owners of the business will not have confidence in the audit report which they issue.

The key point is independence in terms of appearance and mind.

① **Independence of mind.** It is the state of mind that permits the expression of an opinion without being affected by influences that compromise professional judgement, allowing an individual to act with integrity, exercise objectivity and professional skepticism.

② **Independence in appearance.** It is the avoidance of facts and circumstances that are so significant that a reasonable and informed third party would be likely to conclude, weighing all the specific facts and circumstances, that a firm's, or a member of the audit team's, integrity, objectivity, or professional skepticism has been compromised.

11.2.3 Threats to Independence

Self-interest threat: It occurs when the audit firm or a member of the audit team could benefit from a financial interest in, or other self-interest conflicts with an audit client.

Self-review threat: It occurs when the auditor has to evaluate the work again which was completed by himself.

Advocacy threat: It occurs when the auditor is asked to promote the client's position or represent them in some way.

Familiarity threat: It occurs when the auditor is too sympathetic or trusting of the client because of a close relationship with them.

Intimidation threat: The auditor is intimidated to give an unqualified opinion or otherwise

not be re-appointed.

11.3　Standards of Reporting

(1) The report shall state whether the financial statements are presented in accordance with generally accepted accounting principles.

(2) The report shall identify those circumstances in which such principles have not been consistently observed in the current period in relation to the preceding period.

(3) Informative disclosures in the financial statements are to be regarded as reasonably adequate unless otherwise stated in the report.

(4) The report shall either contain an expression of opinion regarding the financial statements, taken as a whole, or an assertion to the effect that an opinion cannot be expressed. When an overall opinion cannot be expressed, the reasons therefore should be stated. In all cases where an auditor's name is associated with financial statements, the report should contain a clear-cut indication of the character of the auditor's work, if any, and the degree of responsibility the auditor is taking.

11.3.1　Unqualified Opinions

The unqualified opinion states that the auditors followed generally accepted auditing standards in the conduct of the audit and that in their opinion the financial statements are fairly presented in accordance with generally accepted accounting principles.

However, conditions may prevent the auditors from completely following generally accepted auditing standards or the auditors may find something during the course of the audit that prevents them from reporting that the financial statements are fair in all respects. In such a case, one of three types of reports other than unqualified is issued: ①a qualified opinion, ②a disclaimer, or ③an adverse opinion.

11.3.2　Qualified Opinions

A qualified opinion states that, with the exception of the qualification or qualifications noted, generally accepted auditing standards were followed and the financial statements are fairly presented in conformity with generally accepted accounting principles. Basically, there are two reasons auditors might issue a qualified opinion.

Firstly, circumstances might prevent them from performing all the audit procedures necessary to follow generally accepted auditing standards. For example, the auditors may not be on hand to observe the count of inventory quantities conducted by the client. If inventory represents a significant portion of total assets (as it often does), the auditors may have to issue a qualified opinion because of the inadequate scope of their audit.

Secondly, during the course of the audit, the auditors may conclude that certain accounting techniques followed by the client are not in accordance with generally accepted accounting principles or that all proper informative disclosures have not been made in the financial statements. In other words, the auditors have conducted the audit in accordance with generally accepted auditing standards and have found omissions or discrepancies that require a qualified opinion.

11.3.3 Disclaimers

A disclaimer states that the scope of the audit is so inadequate that the auditors do not render any opinion on the financial statements, or an uncertainty might have such a serious potential impact on the financial statements that the auditors refuse to give an opinion. The applicable report in these circumstances is one that disclaims an opinion on the financial statements and gives the reasons for so doing. A disclaimer in an auditor's report can have a serious impact on readers' views of the accompanying financial statements. This type of report is therefore rendered only if the auditors are convinced that the inadequate scope or the uncertainty is too serious to warrant a qualified opinion.

11.3.4 Adverse Opinions

An adverse opinion states that, as the result of audit evidence, the auditor concludes that the financial statements taken as a whole are not fairly stated in conformity with generally accepted accounting principles. For example, such a conclusion might be formed because the client records a significant amount of its fixed assets at appraisal value rather than cost.

An adverse opinion, like a disclaimer of opinion, can have a serious effect on the views of readers of the accompanying financial statements. Such an opinion would be issued by the auditors only if they believe that the deviation from generally accepted accounting principles is too serious to warrant a qualified opinion. Modified opinions are shown in Table 11-1.

Table 11-1 Modified opinions

Nature of matter giving rise to the modification	Auditor's judgement about the pervasiveness of the effects or possible effects on the financial statement	
	Material but not pervasive	Material and pervasive
Financial statements are materially misstated	Qualified opinion	Adverse opinion
Auditor unable to obtain sufficient appropriate audit evidence	Qualified opinion	Disclaimer of opinion

Core Words

Planning stage	审计计划阶段
Audit implementation stage	审计实施阶段
Reporting stage	审计报告阶段
Risk assessment	风险评估
Internal control	内部控制
Integrity	真实性
Objectivity	客观性
Professional competence and due care	职业能力和适当关注
Confidentiality	保密性
Professional behavior	职业行为
Independence	独立性
Independence of mind	实质上的独立性
Independence in appearance	形式上的独立性
Unqualified opinion	无保留意见
Qualified opinion	保留意见
Disclaimer of opinion	无法发表审计意见
Adverse opinions	反对意见

Extended Reading

1. 审计的定义

审计是由国家授权或接受委托的专职机构人员，依照国家法规、审计准则和会计准则，运用专门的方法对被审计单位的财政、财务支出、经营管理活动及其相关资料的真实性、正确性、合规性、合法性、效益性进行审查和监督，评价经济责任，鉴证经济业务，用以维护财经法纪、改善经营管理、提高经济效益的一项独立性的经济监督活动。

2. 审计的分类

按审计活动执行主体的性质分类，审计可以分为政府审计、独立审计、内部审计三种。本章介绍的审计指的是外部审计，也就是独立审计。

3. 审计意见的类型

(1) 无保留意见

审计师认为被审计者编制的财务报表已按照适用的会计准则的规定编制，并在所有重大方面公允反映了被审计者的财务状况、经营成果和现金流量。

(2) 保留意见

审计师认为财务报表整体是公允的，但是存在影响重大的错报。

(3) 否定意见

审计师认为财务报表整体是不公允的或没有按照适用的会计准则的规定编制。

(4) 无法表示意见

审计师的审计范围受到了限制，且其可能产生的影响是重大而广泛的，审计师不能获取充分的审计证据。

4. 强调事项段

审计报告的强调事项段是指注册会计师在审计意见段之后增加的对重大事项予以强调的段落。强调事项段应同时符合下列条件：

(1) 可能对财务报表产生重大影响，但被审计单位进行了恰当的会计处理，且在财务报表中做出了充分披露。

(2) 不影响注册会计师发表审计意见。

Exercises

1. Which of the following statements is false? (   )

   A. External audit can also be called independent audit.

   B. The purpose of auditing is to guarantee that there is no error in financial statement.

   C. Auditing cannot help a company to improve profit.

   D. The audit will affect the normal working schedule of enterprise.

2. Which of the following is the advantage of audit? (   )

   A. Disputes between management are easier to resolve.

   B. Major changes in ownership may be facilitated if past accounts contain an unqualified auditing report.

   C. Auditing can help third parties obtain more fair information.

   D. All of the above.

3. Which one is included in the planning stage? (   )

   A. Making audit target.   C. Testing of internal control.

   B. Risk assessment.   D. Audit report.

4. Which one is included in the auditing implementation stage? (   )

   A. Make audit target.   C. Make audit content.

   B. Make audit scope.   D. Make risk assessment.

5. Which one is the final stage of audit? (   )

   A. Help the customer improve profit.

   B. Express an opinion on the financial statement.

   C. Give advice on the strategy of customers.

   D. Help to enhance internal control.

6. Which of the following is not a fundamental principle? (   )

   A. Effectiveness.   C. Objectivity.

   B. Integrity.   D. Confidentiality.

7. Which of the following is not a threat to independence? (   )

   A. Self-review threat.   C. Familiarity threat.

   B. Advocacy threat.   D. Unprofessional threat.

8. Which of the following is not an element of internal control? (   )

A. Control environment.　　　　　C. Control procedure.

B. Risk assessment.　　　　　　　D. Professional behavior.

9. Which is the reflection of the whole audit process during the audit of financial statements of Certified Public Accountants? (   )

A. The audit working paper.　　　　C. The quality of audit work.

B. Audit target.　　　　　　　　　D. Code of professional ethics.

10. All of the following are objectives of internal control except (   ).

A. Maximize net income.　　　　　C. Safeguard assets.

B. Comply with legal requirements.　D. Reliable accounting records.

11. What is the classification of audit?

12. What is the process of auditing?

13. Make an evaluation of this sentence "Audits can help companies maximize profit" and state your opinion with explanation.